I0472899

EQ
THE ENTERPRISE QUOTIENT
Revised Edition

ENTERPRISE - THE SOURCE OF ALL WEALTH

AND

THE STORY OF VENTURE CAPITAL

WITH AN EXPLANATION OF THE CENTRAL ROLE OF INCREASING RETURNS TO SCALE

BY
TIM WALSHAW

Copyright © 2023 Tim Walshaw   All Rights Reserved.

All right reserved. No part of this publication may be reproduced, stored in a retrieval system, or transmitted, in any form or by any means, without the prior permission in writing of the publisher, nor be otherwise circulated in any form or binding or cover than that in which it is published and without a similar condition including this condition being imposed on the subsequent publisher.

ISBN: 978-0-6459786-4-3

Previous related publications by Tim Walshaw:
The Perpetual Inventory Method. **Published 2022.** *The Laffer Curve.* **Published 2021.** *Double Entry Bookkeeping.* **Published 2017.** *Taxing Economic Rents* **Published 2016.** *Increasing Returns to Scale*: *A Simple Way to Make Good Investments, and Not Bad Investments, When Investing in Company Shares.* **Published 2014.** *Economic Rents, the Hidden Profit: How to Find Safe Companies to Invest In.* **Published 2015.**

<publisher Tim Walshaw >
<Canberra, Australia>
<timbot99@gmail.com>

<2023>

Dedicated to

Professor Paul Romer

Nobel Prize Winner in Economics

who finally opened the floodgates for the analysis of increasing returns to scale and was instrumental in causing subsequent fundamental changes in economic analysis, including putting the entrepreneur on the pedestal he should rightfully be, as the creator of all wealth.

CONTENTS

FIGURES

TABLES

EQ - THE ENTERPRISE QUOTIENT

INTRODUCTION

A myriad of myths around the world tell about making money. It is a universal source of fascination. The grindstone that grinds out salt, the soldier who finds gold in a hole in a tree, the hero who finds a cavern full of wealth. This is a subject of attraction. How do I make money? How do I become wealthy?

This book explains what is the source of all wealth.

However, an equal benefit of this book is that it rewrites economic theory at the basic level. For nearly two hundred years economic teaching got stuck in a cul-de-sac – constant returns to scale. And ignored increasing returns to scale. This book shows that constant returns to scale does not exist. From the point of view of correct economic theory, even if the reader has no desire to get rich, this book is extremely valuable.

When I set out to write this book its title was going to be "The Economics of Increasing Returns to Scale". But like all books it took a life of its own, the subject began to change, and it inexorably became "EQ - The Enterprise Quotient". The story of the Entrepreneur, and how closely the success of the Entrepreneur is connected to increasing returns to scale. And why Enterprise is the source of all wealth.

The Entrepreneur is that mysterious but very important person of economics, business and of society as a whole; who, despite his immense importance, on whom nobody in the economics profession has seemed to put a finger on. The man who wasn't there. Like the mysterious prime character in a Noh play that nobody sees.

In fact, in this book there are two characters that are not there.

Everyone sees "Constant Returns to Scale", who is a character that does not exist. But nobody sees the Entrepreneur. The economist William Baumol described the Entrepreneur as the Prince of Denmark who is missing from the play Hamlet. But in reality, the Entrepreneur is the Ghost; out there, pulling the strings, including that of Hamlet. The name of the play is "Increasing Returns to Scale" upon which the major player, the invisible Entrepreneur, operates to rule all the other players.

This book is divided into two parts, Part I and Part II. The first part delves into Microeconomic Theory. For that I apologise to those who would be bored and want to dive into the guts of wealth creation, Enterprise, in Part II. But to do that, we need a complete understanding of that underlying concept of increasing returns to scale.

The reason why the role of Enterprise and the Entrepreneur has not previously been on the central stage of human understanding is that it has been held back by the erroneous theoretical foundation that has hindered human thought for two hundred years. This erroneous theoretical foundation has to be swept away. Nevertheless, if you are impatient and want to know what is the source of all wealth, dive into Part II, then assuage any questions by going back through Part I.

This book starts with a reworking of basic microeconomics, something that should have been done ages ago, and shows that the direction of the supply curve is <u>down</u>, not up, as it is usually supposed. This is because the supply curve reflects increasing returns to scale, which makes the supply curve go down, not up. There is however a small sharp upward movement at the end of the increasing returns curve supply curve, reflecting a short decreasing returns to scale supply curve. There is no, or an infinitely small, constant returns to scale supply curve between the increasing returns to scale and the decreasing returns to scale supply curves.

The Noble Prize-winning economist Paul Romer introduced endogenous growth into the growth function by using knowledge as a non-rival good, and as a consequence he showed that the growth function was non-convex, that is, it exhibits increasing returns. Romer's work will be covered in later chapters, and I will extend his model to introduce the role of the entrepreneur as a cause of growth. While Romer argues that under certain circumstances growth ceases, I have shown that if you introduce the influence of the entrepreneur, you cause unlimited growth.

As I said, I have divided this book into two parts, Part I and Part II. Part I is the theoretical side, and covers Romer's models, and my modifications to his model to include the role of the Entrepreneur. Part II is the practical side. It describes definition of Enterprise, the history of the Entrepreneur, the various definitions, my own merged definition, and description of the entrepreneur's role, and goes onto a description of that new phenomenon, Venture Capital and how it works.

These two parts ought to be read together. I know many have no interest in economic theory, but reading of Part I leads to a better understanding of Part II. On the other hand, many economists may be disappointed by the lack of mathematics in Part I, but I have tried to keep the use of mathematics to a minimum. If you want more mathematics, go to Romer's work.

The purpose of this book has been to thrust the role of Enterprise, and the role of the Entrepreneur, out onto the centre of the stage, and turn the spotlight onto entrepreneurial activity. The related purpose of this book is to change the teaching of economics, and move it out from the blind alley it has got itself into — constant returns to scale, the upward sloping supply curve, equilibrium, pure competition; and all that plethora of related nonsensical economic theory such as general equilibrium, input output, and of course Marxism, that has little use (no, Marxism is not useful) except to provide lifetime employment for academic economists.

However, I have also a final desire. That many reading this book learn that they can make a lot of money. The scales fall from their eyes, and they see how easy it is to become an entrepreneur, and the benefits of becoming an entrepreneur. The entrepreneur, together with enterprise, is the source of all wealth, for themselves and for society as a whole. The final conclusion of this book is that a nation's prosperity and growth depend on the number of entrepreneurs, as well as their activities. The more entrepreneurs in the economy there are, and the more enterprise there is, the better off everybody is. Entrepreneurs should be encouraged as fundamental government policy, as they are the sole source of economic growth and economic welfare; not discouraged through ideological antagonism.

PART I

REVISING MICROECONOMIC THEORY AND THE THEORY OF INCREASING RETURNS

CHAPTER ONE

SUPPLY AND DEMAND

It is necessary to start by going back to nearly first principles in Economic theory. Nearly everyone is familiar with the Supply-Demand diagram. In this diagram the Demand curve goes in the downward direction, as when price falls, the quantity demanded increases. Supply is said to go in the opposite direction – the quantity supplied increases as the price increases. It is all a matter of economic incentives. Where these lines cross is the market price. This somewhat trite but compelling argument is at the core of economics. It is illustrated in Figure 1 below.

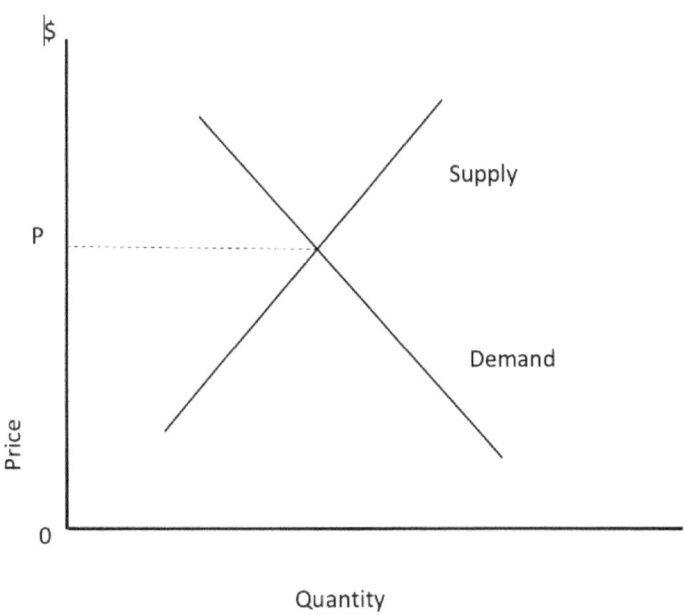

Figure 1   The Supply and Demand Line Diagram

The above diagram shows the conventional supply/demand diagram. Demand is sloping down to the right. Supply slopes upwards to the left. Where they intersect is the equilibrium price. This is the standard diagram taught to every economics student. When the lecturer crosses the supply and demand line, students are told "From now in, you are economists!"

That is all very well. Very comforting for trainee economists. But that diagram is not correct. For a start, this analysis encourages students to think that this diagram of Supply and Demand in markets is the same for individual firms. Nothing could be further than the truth. Furthermore, the student is not taught that marginal revenue, not the demand line, which is average revenue, sets the price when crossed by the supply line.

Back to a bit more analysis of Demand. For both the market and for individual firms, as firms face market demand, the demand line is average revenue, and there is a line also for marginal revenue. This will be explained in detail in the next chapter, but these lines are shown in the next Figure 2. Now, as these lines describe both market demand, and also the demand for the products of an individual firm.

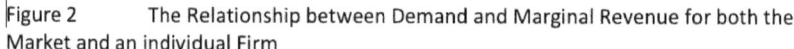
Figure 2   The Relationship between Demand and Marginal Revenue for both the Market and an individual Firm

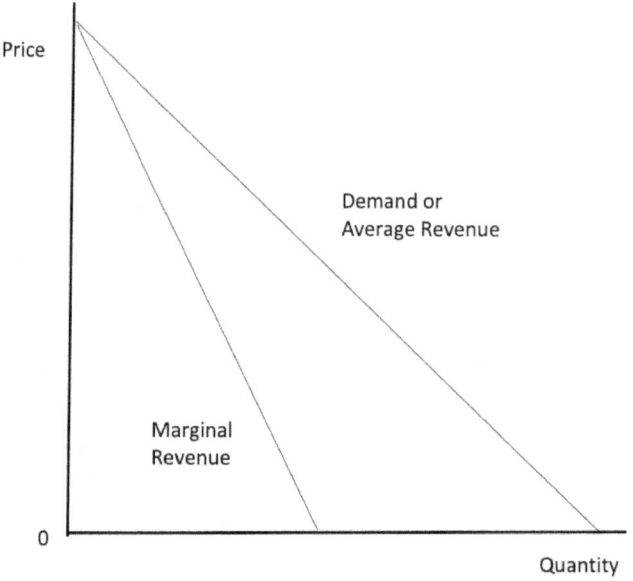

Now we move to an individual firm. We assume initially that it has an upward sloping supply curve for its product. One of the basic assumptions of microeconomics is that in this case as the price for the product increases the firm produces more, (demand driven), or more accurately, as production increases the firm can only sell at higher prices (supply driven). As will be seen later this assumes what is called 'decreasing returns to scale'. However, there is such a property of supply curves called 'increasing returns to scale'. Both decreasing returns to scale and increasing returns to scale will be discussed in detail in forthcoming chapters.

The question of demand driven or supply driven supply goes back to the roots of economics. However, you can only have demand driven supply when you have an upwardly sloping demand curve. Downward sloping supply goes with falling prices.

In Figure 3, it shows a firm where a firm's upwardly climbing supply curve crosses the market demand curve.

Figure 3 .... The Firm's Supply Line the Firm's Marginal Revenue Line and the Market Demand Line

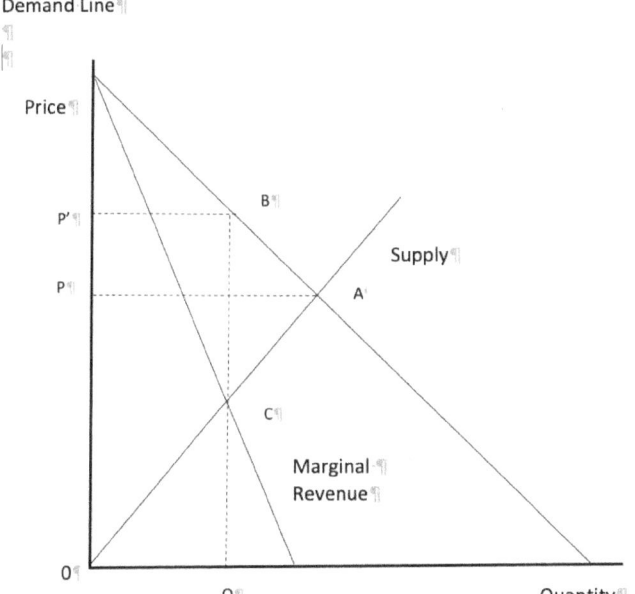

But what is equilibrium price for the firm? It is at the intersection of the Supply and Demand line, point A. At the

market equilibrium, total profit is zero. At this point the equilibrium price is P.

But when the firm makes a profit. The price is at P'.

In reality, all economic analysis should be about when the firm makes a profit. The analysis of firms when they make zero profit, the so-called equilibrium, is in the opinion of the author, is a useless cul-de-sac.

Conventional thinking says that the equilibrium price P is shown in Figure 1. The argument is that under perfect competition there are a large number of firms with a horizontal Demand line meeting an upward sloping Supply line, as shown in Figure 4. These lines are said to aggregate to figure 1 when aggregated.

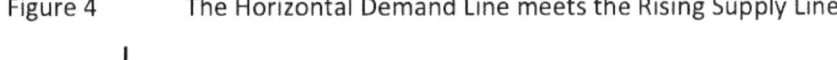

Figure 4   The Horizontal Demand Line meets the Rising Supply Line

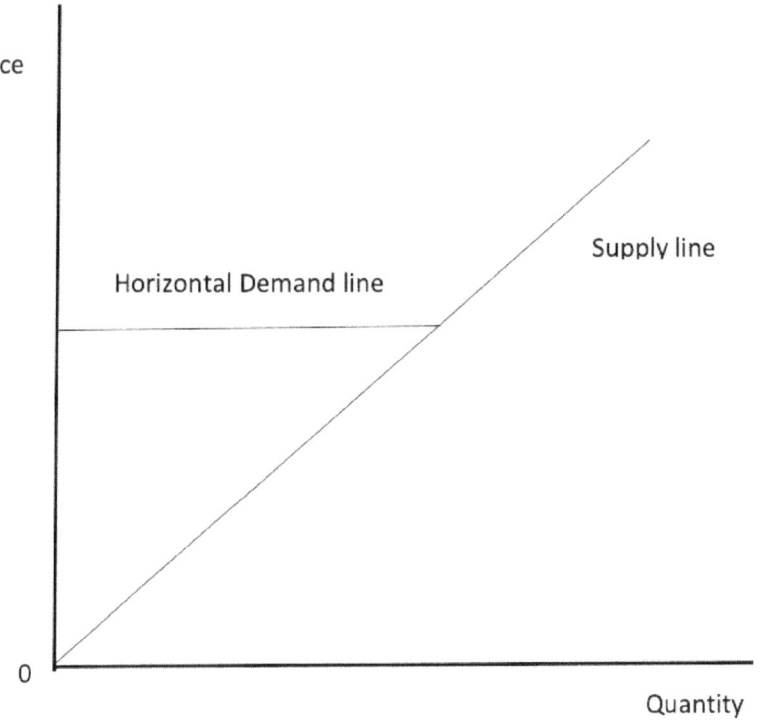

In fact, it is the opposite that happens. Under perfect competition, there is <u>infinite Supply</u>, yet market Demand is unaffected. The true situation is that there is a large number of firms with the supply/demand position of Figure 3, and when aggregated under perfect competition, the market appears to have an infinite supply and unchanged demand, as in Figure 5. The horizontal Supply line meets the downward sloping Demand line.

Figure 5   The Horizontal Supply Line meets the downward sloping Demand Line

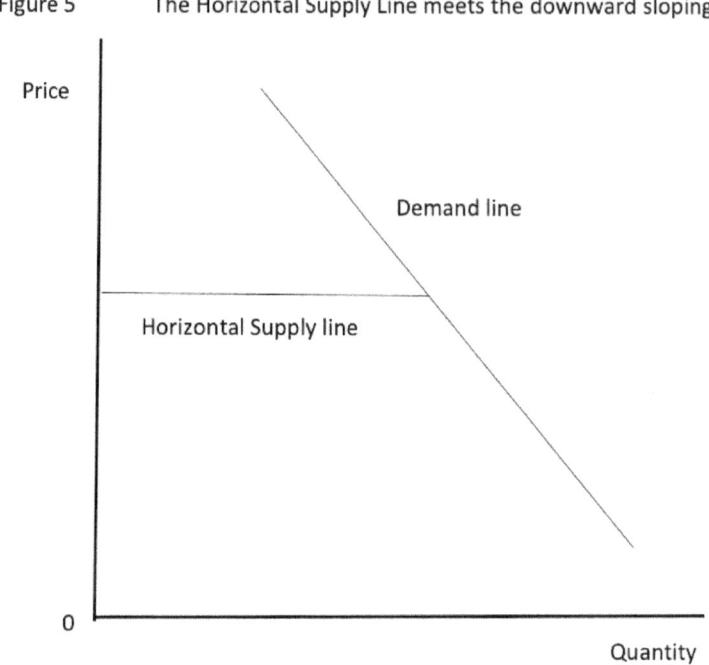

This diagram shows the final market equilibrium Supply/Demand diagram, not Figure 1. All textbooks need to be rewritten!

The basic fault with the previous standard theory is that it assumes that perfect competition is perfect competition among the *buyers/demanders*, leading to a flat demand line. But It is perfect competition among the *suppliers*. An infinite number of supplying firms are competing among themselves. This leads to a flat supply line as the inefficient firms are eliminated, and the remaining firms decide competitively among themselves what is the minimum price that that they can sell the maximum amount goods they can supply.

In effect the market is divided into a maximum quantity that can be sold at various prices (there is not infinite demand). Each supplier can supply a certain amount at a given price. Thus, the total supply is divided into quantities supplied by the individual firms. So, there is a trade-off between the total quantity supplied by the individual firms, (they divide up the total supply in Figure 5) and the price. As in Figure 5, this flat total supply line is truncated by the demand line.

To summarise. Under the old theory, under perfect competition the market demand line intersects with market supply, as in Figure 1, that gives a market price P. For an individual firm it faces a flat *demand* curve at price P, for which it produces at a fixed quantity Q.

In the new theory, the direction of causation is the opposite. Perfect competition among firms leads to a flat *supply* curve. All individual firms supply at the same price, regardless of the quantity they produce. This is shown in Figure 5. There are an infinite number of possible firms. If a firm cannot supply at this price it drops out. If the firm can supply at this price, it supplies the maximum quantity it can produce in a market constrained by the demand line. This is aggregated to a flat supply line for the for the total quantity supplied at a certain price. This supply line is constrained by a downward sloping market demand line that is unaffected by perfect competition among the suppliers. This is the perfectly competitive market diagram.

A frequent story told at this level of microeconomics is that of the farmer, who is compelled to sell into the market at a certain demand market price, over which he has no control. This is an erroneous inference of the situation. In reality, farmers as a whole do control the market situation, and collectively set the supply price. There is a fixed demand, set by the market, with a sloping demand line. Then the individual farmers decide how much they can produce, and the minimum price they will sell to the market of various quantities they are willing to sell. This is not necessarily the maximum quantity they can produce (though there could be feedback from the expected market price). For the rest, they will have alternative uses – seed, stock feed, consumption etc. So, the aggregate flat supply line at a certain price is 'chopped up' by the various farmers, who sell onto the market some or all their product at that price. The *total* quantity supplied is truncated by the market demand line, and that provides the market price. Again, see Figure 5.

As an aside, in economics it is mainly about supply. It is supply that mostly matters. Not Demand. But up to recently, economic theory has concentrated on Demand, and this has led to a concentration on Demand in Macroeconomic policy, with harmful effects. If the policy emphasis became on Supply, say on the supply of money, increasing supply in recessions (Say's Law), not demand, economic policy making would be far more effective.

I know this conclusion contradicts accepted economic theory, and there is probably a strong ideological requirement to have a horizontal *demand* line in the theory of perfect competition. Yes, Keynes said increase Demand in a recession. But a little thought will show that the Supply line, not the Demand line, that is flat. The standard argument says that under perfect competition there has to be perfect competition in market demand, not supply, but even under perfect competition the competition is not among the demanders, but the suppliers. Market demand is unaffected by increased competition among the suppliers as market demand is separate from the behaviour of the suppliers. There may be only a few in the market to purchase goods. The competition is among the suppliers of goods, and as this competition increases it can become perfect competition. Many thousands of nearly identical firms are selling into the same market.

Why is the purely competitive market Supply line horizontal? In the purely competitive world, there are an infinite number of firms selling with both decreasing returns to scale and increasing returns to scale, as well as constant returns to scale. Assuming that in this infinite number of firms there are an equal number of firms operating under decreasing returns to scale and increasing returns to scale, the values of the slopes cancel each other out when the values of the slopes are aggregated, leaving the flat horizontal line of the sum of the constant returns to scale – in a perfect market only! Not for individual firms. As will be seen later, the vast majority must operate under increasing returns to scale in practice.

If it can somehow be argued that in this perfectly competitive world there are a different number of firms operating under a decreasing or increasing returns to scale, then there would be a slope in the supply line. But this outcome is not likely.

Due to infinite competition, the aggregate Supply curve is horizontal. All firms sell at a single price into the market. So, it is the Supply curve that is horizontal, not the Demand curve, under perfect competition.

CHAPTER TWO

MARGINAL REVENUE, MARGINAL COSTS AND PROFITS

Profits are NOT Demand less Supply, the difference between the Supply and Demand line in Figure 1. As Supply is the Marginal Cost line, Profits are *Marginal Revenue minus Marginal Costs*, or Marginal Revenue minus Supply. In economics the Demand line is superfluous for analysis. Its sole interest is part of that demand and supply diagram, Price being said to be set at the crossing point. But, as been described in the previous chapter in Figure 3, price is set when Supply crosses the Marginal Revenue line, and is vertically above this point at the Demand line.

Some readers might say that I am being unnecessarily pedantic. This is only theory. Who cares? First, it is my desire that all these economic textbooks are corrected. But more importantly, this theory forms the building blocks of all economics (including all that mathematical stuff). If you get it wrong, it does not work. This is probably the fundamental reason why so many macroeconomic analyses don't work. As I said previously, economics is all about Supply – not Demand.

We next discuss marginal revenue, shown in Figure 6. Yes, we have discussed this before, but as this leads on to other important issues, it is worth repeating in more detail.

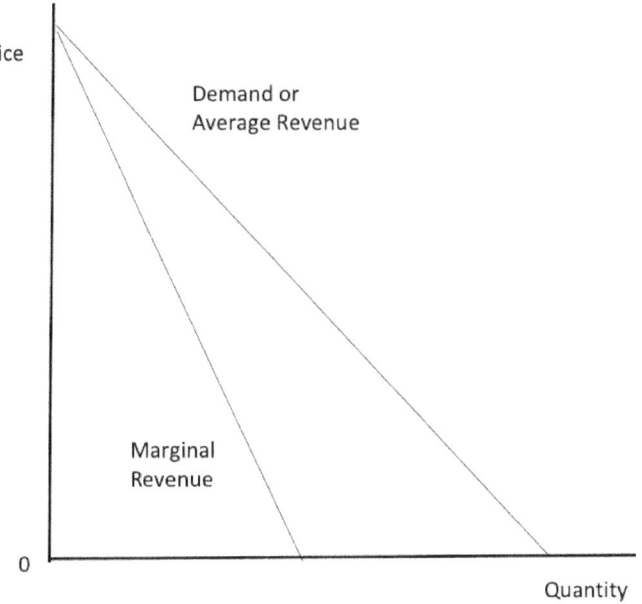

Figure 6 shows two lines, the market Demand line and the firm's Marginal Revenue line. The Demand line is the Average Revenue line. The Demand line shows the price for a commodity, and Price is Revenue at a point divided by Quantity at that point. Revenue divided by quantity is Price, or Average Revenue. The Demand line shows the price offered for every Quantity. As the Price declines Quantity demanded increases.

Why is Demand the same as Average Revenue? Demand is the price for a good at any quantity sold. Total Revenue is Price x Quantity. For Average Revenue you divide by Quantity, which is Price. Thus Demand = Price = Average Revenue.

Average Revenue/Demand Price declines as Quantity sold increases. (Though occasionally in the real-world Price can increase faster than Quantity supplied, but this is highly unusual – a famine or the equivalent).

The differential of Total Revenue is Marginal Revenue. Marginal Revenue is the marginal decline in revenue as each marginal increase in quantity. It starts at zero when quantity is zero. If the Demand line is straight it can be shown that the value of Marginal Revenue at any quantity Q is half the Average Revenue.

The Marginal Revenue line starts where the Market Demand line crosses the 'y' axis, when the firm's quantity of production is zero, and is the firm's Marginal Revenue line. Thus, while the quantity demanded is set by the market, the marginal revenue is set by the production capacity of the firm.

Now we introduce the Supply line. The Supply line is also the Marginal Cost line, and (under decreasing returns to scale) is upward sloping to the right. Under decreasing returns to scale, as quantity produced increases marginally, the cost also increases marginally. As shown in figure 3, this upward sloping Marginal Cost line crosses the Marginal Revenue line. Again, these quantities are set by the individual firm.

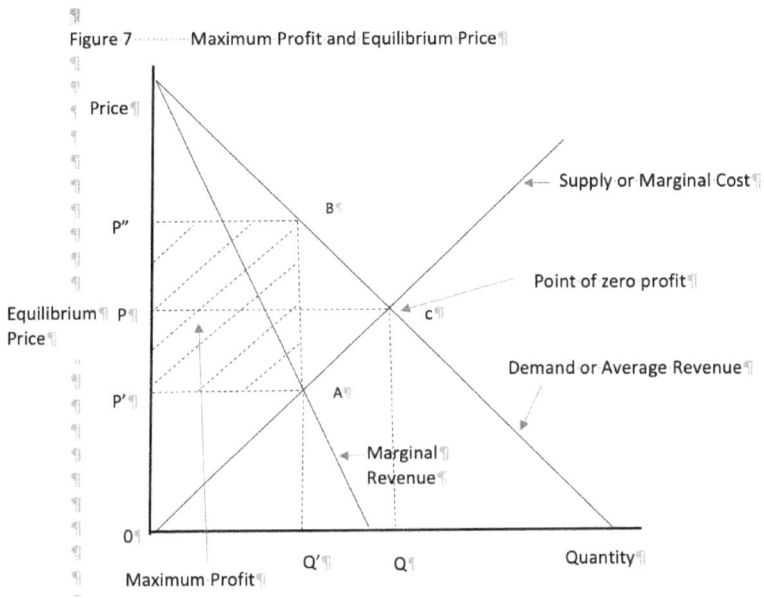

Figure 7 ········· Maximum Profit and Equilibrium Price

Maximum profit is where Marginal Revenue = Marginal Cost at A.

Maximum Profit is (P – P') x Q.

Going towards Q from Q', approaches B, and B – A approaches 0.

Therefore, at Q, Profit is B – A x Q

Or   0   x Q

Therefore, at C, total profit is zero.

At the equilibrium point C, total profit is 0.

It should be pointed out, that while Supply – Demand diagram extends the Supply line above C, this should not be done. This is because the firm makes zero profit beyond this point, and would therefore not supply goods beyond point C. The correct figure is shown in Figure 8.

Again, this diagram does not explain pure competition, as the firm makes a profit up to point C. Pure competition is the diagram with the flat Supply curve, as in Figure 5.

From here on, when the term equilibrium is mentioned, it refers to "equilibrium for the firm", that is when the firm's profit is zero. For market equilibrium, refer to Figure 5, were the flat Supply line ceases when profits are zero for that market. It is necessary to differentiate between market equilibrium and individual firm equilibrium. Standard economics tends to be vague on this issue.

In Figure 8, we introduce the role of profits.

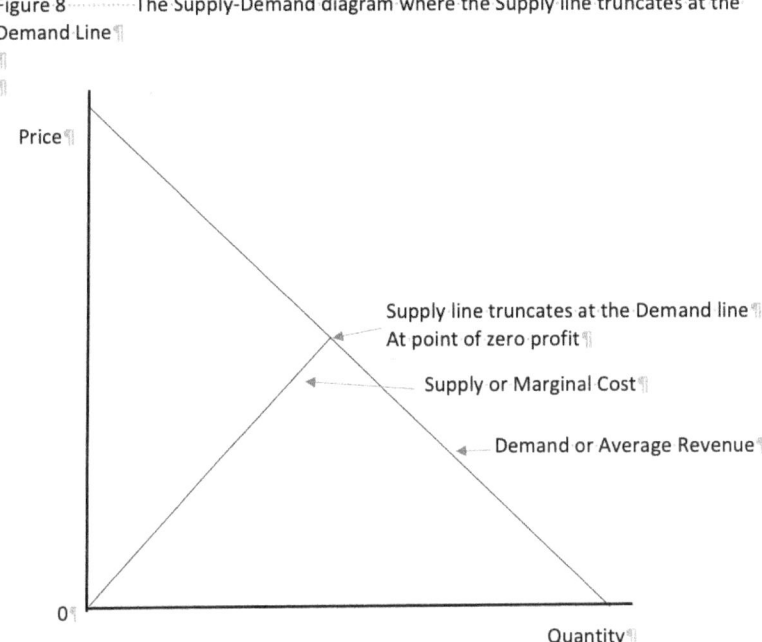

Figure 8 .... The Supply-Demand diagram where the Supply line truncates at the Demand Line

On the question of the supply line

But most markets sell goods that are continuously produced. And yes, there is a supply line. However, that upward sloping supply line is only one of the possible supply lines. The supply lines illustrated in Figure 1 and Figure 3 shows just one of them – decreasing returns to scale. Three others are possible with different shapes (discussed later). These are increasing returns to scale, and constant returns to scale. And there is a vertical supply line, which is the supply for a fixed quantity.

Is equilibrium economics relevant?

For many years, economists have been obsessed by equilibrium economics, and only in the past decades have a few progressive radical economists have been talking about the possibility of disequilibrium economics. In fact, equilibrium economics is only a tiny fraction of the total possibilities in the real world. It is just a few restricted markets trading in a fixed quantity of good or products, such as share markets or wholesale markets for vegetables. The vast majority of any economy is firms selling goods continuously being manufactured or produce, for a profit. Such markets operate continuously in disequilibrium to make a profit, mostly in increasing returns to scale and a minority in decreasing returns to scale. To operate in equilibrium the continuously operating producer must make zero profits, see Figure 8 above, as the equilibrium price is set when there is zero profits, when the supply line crosses the marginal revenue line.

I concede that (if the theory is correct – See Figure 5) perfect competition models are a useful teaching tool. But the teacher should get students onto reality as fast as possible. Economists should be trained to provide useful and practical advice to people with economics questions. Not have their heads filled with nonsensical theories. Accounting consultants may not be correct much of the time, but at least their advice is more realistic, and indeed safer, than current economists' advice.

CHAPTER THREE

THE MARKET FOR FIXED SUPPLY

At this point we diverge for a moment to the important markets where there is fixed supply. There is no continuous production. There is just a vertical supply line.

As such, as can be seen in Figure 9 below, the Price is at the intersection of the vertical Supply line and the Demand line. This is at point B, that is vertically above point A, the intercept of the Supply and Marginal Revenue lines.

Such markets are common. They are markets for commodities with fixed and not continuous supply, such as land, shares, bonds, houses and so on.

Conceptually if supply is fixed, and if Demand is fixed, there will be a fixed constant price. In practice, the Demand line moves around. Also, the quantity supplied to the market varies with time. As a consequence, the price moves up and down.

In markets where fixed quantities are sold, the supply line can be said to be redundant. These quantities are sold up and down the Demand line. This is the market where there is no variable production of the goods sold.

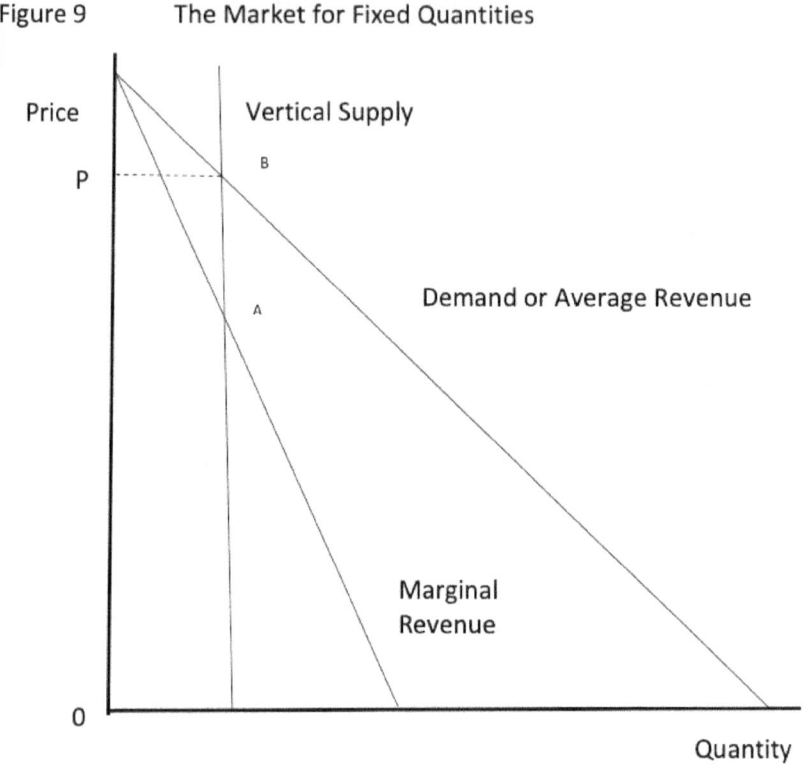

Figure 9   The Market for Fixed Quantities

Price

Vertical Supply

P

B

Demand or Average Revenue

A

Marginal
Revenue

0

Quantity

In Figure 9, there is a single downward sloping Demand line, but unlike in Figure 1, there is no upward sloping Supply line. There is no continuous supply. Just these fixed quantities. Of course, this does not imply that the Demand line stays fixed in place. It continuously moves around, and as a result the price varies widely for a standard quantity sold.

CHAPTER FOUR

AN EXPLANATION OF THE CONCEPTS 0F INCREASING, DECREASING AND CONSTANT RETURNS TO SCALE USING STRAIGHT LINE DIAGRAMS

Moving on the discuss Supply.

Since the fundamental theme of this book is "increasing returns to scale", it is best that we don't proceed until we have defined the concept.

Idealized straight line diagrams of the returns to scale concepts are shown in Figures 10, 11 and 12, all under the heading of "The Straight Line Explanation of Increasing, Decreasing and Constant Returns to Scale",

Starting with Figure 10, Increasing Returns to Scale, diagram (a), has output on the 'y' axis and input on the "x" axis. This diagram shows a straight line with a positive slope growing at a slope greater than 45%. This indicates that for a firm, output increases faster than input.

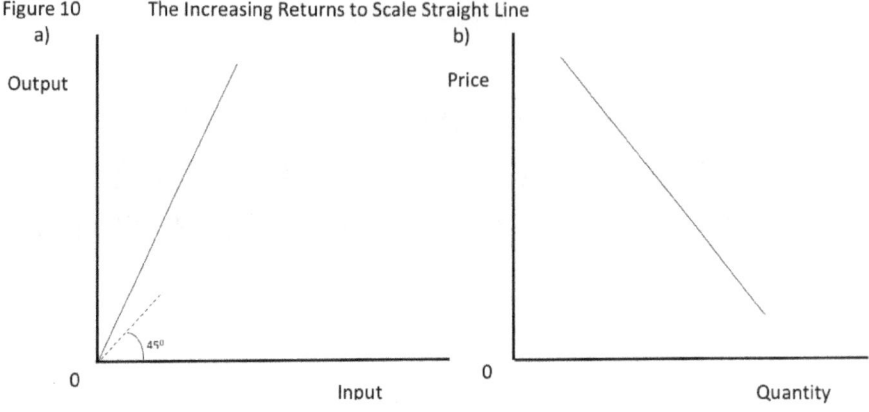

Figure 10   The Increasing Returns to Scale Straight Line

This diagram is translated to diagram (b), where the "y" axis is the price and the "x" axis is the quantity, via an increasing marginal product curve (not shown due to lack of space). Output increases faster than input. Then the ratio of output to input increases. If this product has a unit price, then the marginal price declines. Since we are looking at the supply price, this marginal price becomes the marginal cost.

In diagram (b) the 'y' axis is price and the 'x' axis is quantity. If output is assumed to have a unit cost price, the diagram (a) is translated in diagram (b), but with the marginal cost line having a negative slope.

The marginal cost line is also called the Supply Line in economic terminology. A *declining* Supply line is called, confusingly, Increasing Returns to Scale. This is because it is directly related to an increasing Total Product line increasing at a rate steeper than 45 degrees.

26

We now move on to Figure 11, Decreasing Returns to Scale. All the axes in Figures 10, 11 and 12 have the same axes and structure so the explanation will now speed up.

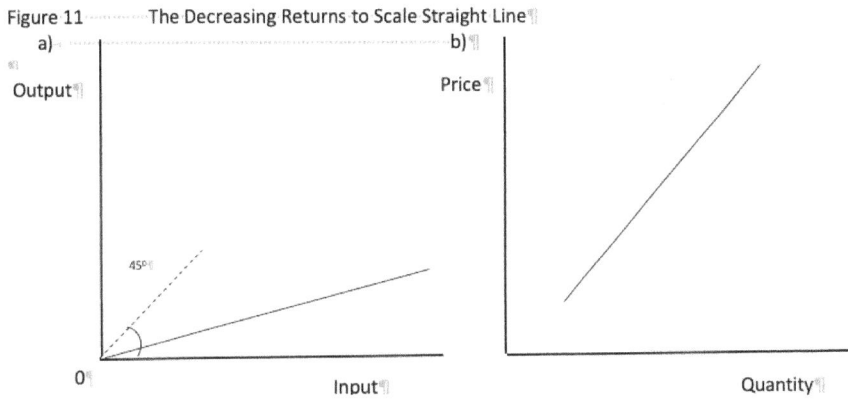

Figure 11 ....The Decreasing Returns to Scale Straight Line

a)

Output

b)

Price

45°

0

Input

Quantity

In Diagram (a) in Figure 11 the product line has a slope less than 45% that implies decreasing returns to scale. Unit output is growing less fast than unit input. This translates to a marginal product line with a slope less than 45 degrees and a rising marginal cost line or Supply Curve. A *rising* Supply Curve means decreasing returns to scale.

Finally, constant returns to scale in Figure 12. In Diagram (a), the output line rises at 45%. This implies the ratio of output to input is constant. This translates to a flat marginal cost or Supply line in Diagram (b). The ratio of marginal cost to quantity supplied is constant.

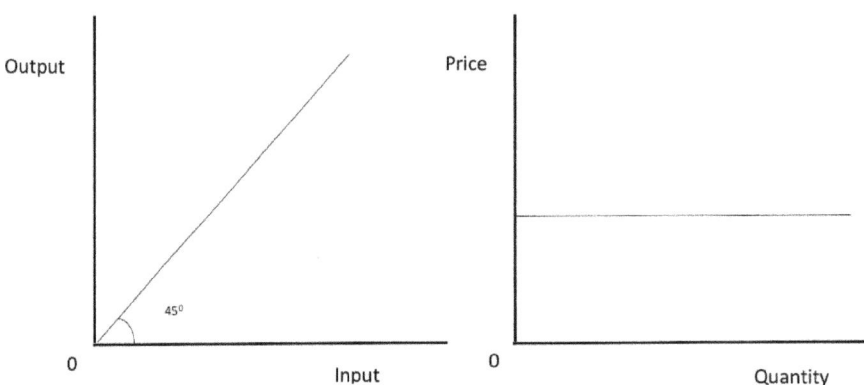

Figure 12   The Constant Returns to Scale Straight Line

These three Supply curves are technically the only continuous Supply curves geometrically possible. The vertical supply line previously discussed is not a continuous supply line.

However, as will be discussed later, the Constant Returns to Scale Supply Curve does not exist, or exists only for a minute fraction of the number of firms – basically firms with a maximum of one or two employees. This has major implications for economic theory.

CHAPTER FIVE

THE CURVED GEOMETRY OF VARIOUS RETURNS TO SCALE

In this chapter we will develop the economic theory of supply, get away from those straight lines and fixed quantities, and bring greater reality into this economic discussion.

The reason why we are doing this is to both move away from the straight lines of the previous chapters, and also the move into the price-quantity world from the straight quantity in – quantity out world. The ultimate reason will come apparent shortly.

When you get to curved lines, geometrically, there only three possible forms of (continuous) Supply:
1. Concave up, called in economics Increasing Returns to Scale
2. Concave down, called in economics Decreasing Returns to Scale
3. Straight line. Called in economics Constant Returns to Scale

This assumes Supply has only a positive growth rate, that is they go upwards, and these three lines always have a positive growth, not negative growth, or constant growth. (The latter two slopes are possible, but we are talking about realistic functioning economies).

The above three possibilities are a geometric axiom. Like the axioms of Euclid.

We have now moved on from quantities on both axes. The axes are now price on the 'y' axis and quantity of the 'x' axis.

The above three types of curves can be shown in the form of the following diagrams:

Figure 13   The Concave Up Total Product Curve, or Increasing Returns to Scale

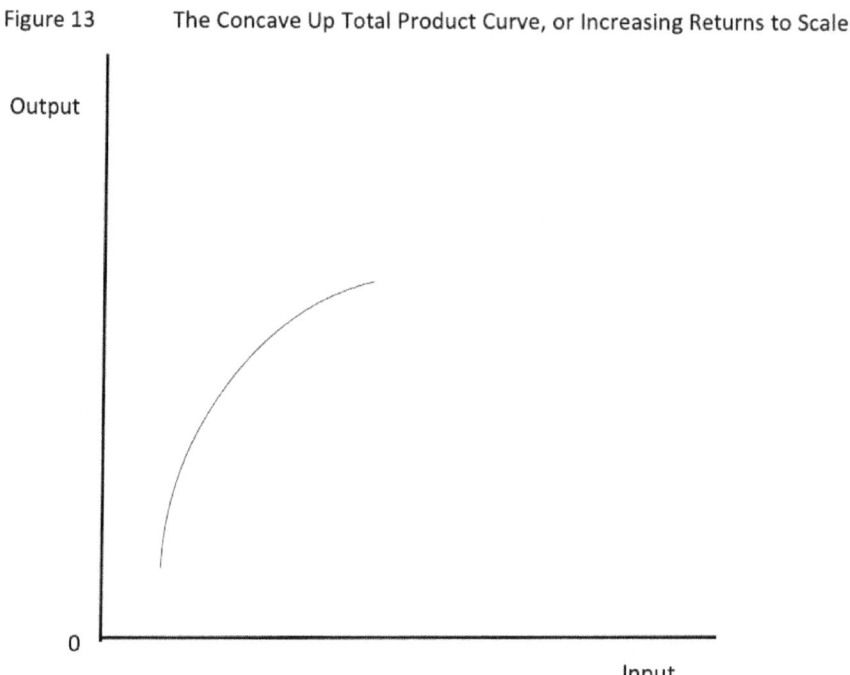

As can be seen, the Increasing Returns to Scale supply curve is a curve that slopes upward at a faster rate than the rate of supply of inputs. Geometrically this is called concave up. The reason why this process is called increasing returns to scale is because the quantity of output increases at a faster rate in relative terms to the quantity of input.

The second diagram has the opposite shaped curve, and is shown in Figure 14.

Figure 14   The Concave Down Total Product Curve, or Decreasing Returns to Scale

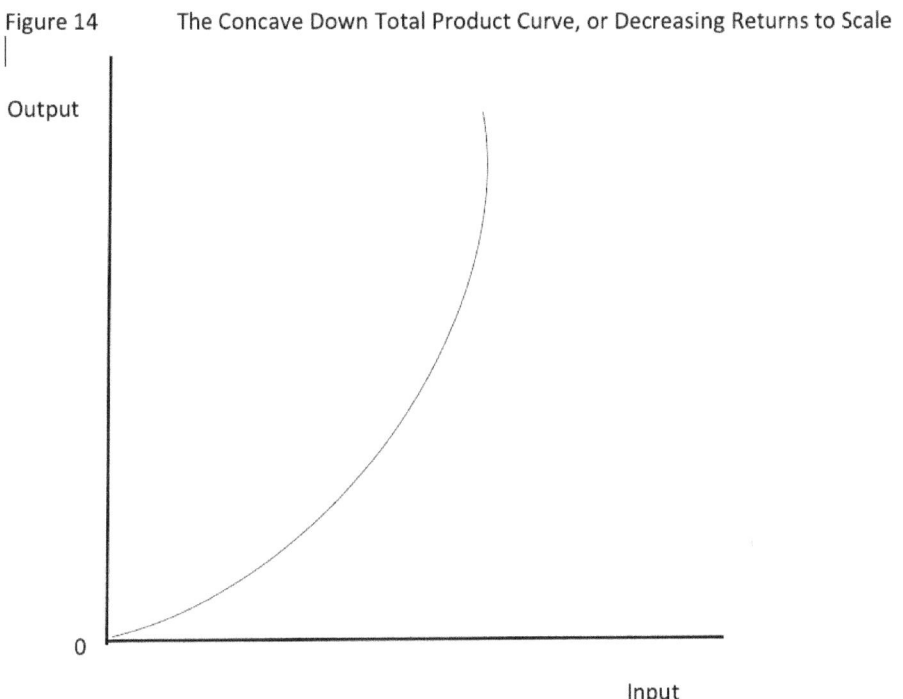

As can be seen, the decreasing returns to scale curve is a curve that slopes upwards at a slower rate. Geometrically it is called concave down. In economics it is called Decreasing Returns to Scale, as the quantity of output decreases at a faster rate in relation to the quantity of input.

The third figure is a Straight Line, or Constant Returns to Scale. This is shown in the diagram in Figure 15.

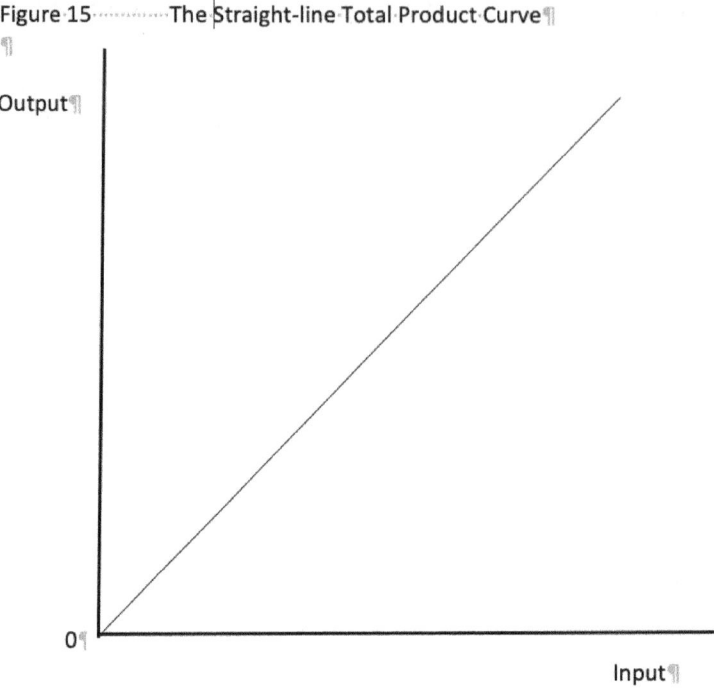

Figure 15········· The Straight-line Total Product Curve

Output

0

Input

Figure 15 shows that the quantity of output increases at the same rate as the quantity of input. This straight line can have any slope, but at that rate of increase the ratio of output to input does not change.

Looking at that line, it can be seen how artificial this construct is. A firm could easily fall off this trajectory and not return. In fact, so called "knife edge" theories, having the basic assumption of constant returns to scale, say this.

As an aside, it is amazing how much of economic theory has been built on the theory of constant returns to scale. This goes back historically to the beginnings of economic theory, but there are large areas of economics, such as general

32

equilibrium theory, input-output theory, and indeed Marxist economic theory, that are dependent on the assumption of constant returns to scale.

From now on, this discussion gets slightly more complex, as it moves to greater realism. It will be seen later in this book, only one form of production is possible, increasing returns to scale. Decreasing returns to scale is very limited, and only happens when the firm ceases to operate under increasing returns to scale, and management hits the wall. Constant returns to scale is confined to very small firms, with fewer than two or three employees, such as small retailers. They cannot grow. This area of small business forms a very small proportion of the economy in aggregate.

CHAPTER SIX

JOINING THE TOTAL PRODUCT CURVES

In order to obtain a better explanation of the product process in the real world, the Increasing Returns curve in Figure 13 and the Decreasing Returns Curve in Figure 14 are joined to form the so called 'S' curve. Also called a Sigmoid curve or a Logistic curve.

Yes, geometrically there are other possible combinations of the increasing returns, decreasing returns and constant returns to scale curves. But the other combinations are not economically realistic. Business economics has totally chosen the 'S' curve against any other possibilities. The universal assumption is that growth is slow at first, then it speeds up, and the it slows down. If you ask "Why should growth follow this pattern?". "Can't growth start out fast, the slow down, and then speed up again?", or alternatively "Can variable growth be interspersed with constant growth?", the answer is no. It is all to do with the cumulative rate of learning, and how it interacts with technology, production and output, and accumulated inefficiencies later in the growth phase. There has been a massive discussion on the 'S' curve. Most just explain it without question. A few give reasons why the alternatives don't exist. I good summary of this discussion is *'S-Curve Analysis'* in *"Strategy in 3D"* by Greg Fisher, John E Warnock and Rene M. Bakker, 2020.

There is not enough space in this book to provide such a discussion. The reader will have to accept that the 'S' curve is all the happens in the business world. The other possibilities do not occur at all in the real world.

The next diagram, Figure 16, shows the joining of the Increasing Returns to Scale curve, in Figure 13 with the Decreasing Returns to Scale curve in Figure 14 to make the 'S' curve or the logistic curve.

Figure 16   Joining the increasing returns and decreasing returns to scale total product curves to become a logistic curve

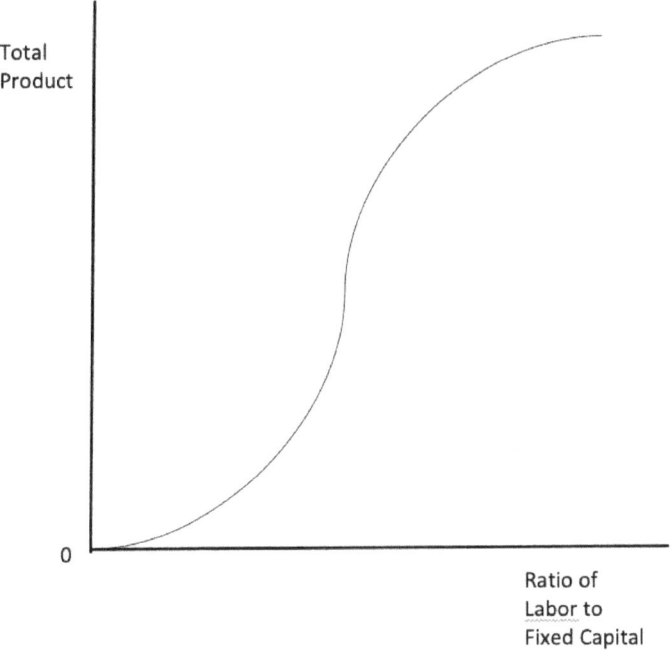

In the above Figure 16, increasing returns to scale comes first, and it is then joined by the decreasing returns to scale curve. This is the so called 'S' curve.

Growth of the product starts at zero, and at first grows gradually. As growth continues the growth rate accelerates until it reaches a maximum. The curve is convex upwards. The curve then passes an inflexion point and growth begins to slow down. Growth becomes slower and slower, until growth ceases. This curve is concave downwards.

In economic usage, when the total product curve is concave upwards, the firm is operating under increasing returns to scale. When the total product curve is concave down the firm is operating under decreasing returns to scale.

While constant returns to scale is at the inflexion point, it is very small, and it can be seen on this diagram that the firm operates only in increasing returns to scale or decreasing returns to scale. Empirical work described in Chapter Fourteen shows that no large firms operate under constant returns to scale. The area of constant returns to scale is too unstable for large firms to operate in.

The only firms that can possibly operate under constant returns to scale are very small firms such as small retailers, with a couple of employees. As will be seen later, such firms are constrained to remain small and cannot expand. They rapidly reach a profit limit. Such very small firms are economically if not numerically a very small part of the aggregate economy.

CHAPTER SEVEN

THE GROWTH OF THE FIRM

Let's start at the very basis of economics, going back to Adam Smith's book *Wealth of Nations.* The growth of the firm. This can be described by the growth rate of the firm's total product. Take a simple model of the firm's inputs and outputs.

It is rare for the economics lecturer to describe how the supply curve is derived. If this is done, the process leads to major surprises. So, take a step back. Compare the growth of output in a simplified diagram with the quantity of input. There must be a whole range of inputs that go into that output. Let's narrow it down to one variable input, Labor, L, and assume away for now all other variable inputs. Assume the other major input, Capital, K, is constant. This is a very simple model, but it can be seen that other variable inputs would follow the same model.

Draw a diagram with total product, Q, on the 'y' axis and total input l/K on the 'x' axis. Now what would this relationship be? A straight line? While in the past, economist have been happy with this simplification, modern economic analysis has brought in an attempt at greater reality.

It has been well established experience that that the firm's economic growth usually takes the form of an 'S' curve. See Figure 16 above. Growth of product starts at zero, and at first it grows gradually. As growth continues, this growth in the rate of the product accelerates, until it reaches a maximum. This curve is concave upwards.

The curve then passes an inflection point and growth begins to slow down. The growth becomes slower and slower, until the curve is flat. This curve is concave downwards. Yes, this is a repeat of the latter part of Chapter Six, but the purpose is to introduce the economic concept of total product, and the Total Product Curve.

As can be seen in Figure 16, initially total product increases at a faster rate, and the curve is concave upwards. Then the rate of growth of the total product begins to slow, and the curve is concave downwards.

In economic usage, when the total product curve is concave upwards, the firm is operating under increasing returns to scale. This is when the rate of increase of total product output is faster than the rate of labor input. When the total product curve is concave down the firm is operating under decreasing returns to scale. This when the rate of increase of total product output is slower than the rate of increase of labor input. This is shown in Figure 17.

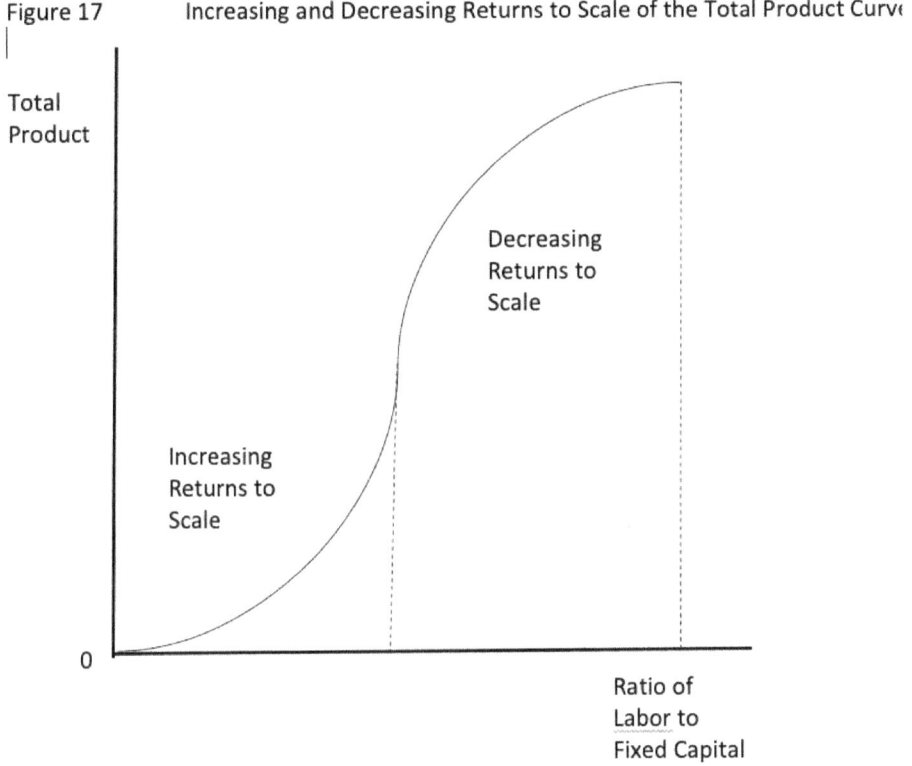

Figure 17   Increasing and Decreasing Returns to Scale of the Total Product Curve

Total Product

Decreasing Returns to Scale

Increasing Returns to Scale

0

Ratio of Labor to Fixed Capital

Increasing returns to scale is the concave upward part of the curve where the rate of growth of output the rate of growth of input.

Decreasing returns to scale is the concave downward part of the curve where the rate of growth or output is less than the rate of growth of input.

Constant returns to scale is at the inflection point. It is very small, and as can be seen the firm operates only in increasing returns to scale or decreasing returns to scale. There is no extended period where the firm operates under constant returns to scale.

In the real world it has been found that few if any firms operate with constant returns to scale. Empirical research described in Chapter Fourteen describes that all the firms analysed in the data set also operate in either increasing returns to scale or decreasing returns to scale. No firm operates in precisely constant returns to scale, though many operate in the region but with increasing or decreasing returns to scale.

CHAPTER EIGHT

DERIVING THE AVERAGE PRODUCT AND MARGINAL PRODUCT CURVES

From this Total Product curve can be derived the Marginal Product and the Average Product curves. The marginal product is the rate of growth of the Total Product curve. The average product is the total product at any point divided by the amount of labor input at that point. A marginal product can be found by the differential of the formula of the total product curve.

The Total Product curve can be more closely defined using a formula. Another name for the Logistic curve is the 'Sigmoid curve', or as it is commonly called, an 'S Curve'. The "y" axis is Total Product Q and the "x" axis is the ratio of Labor to Fixed Capital, L/K. Sigmoid curves are heavily used in business analysis to measure the growth rate of sales of a new product. It is also used in microbial biology to measure the growth rate of microbes in Petri dish. In a large number of applications, the concept is very useful.

A simple general formula of a Sigmoid curve is:

$$S(x) = \frac{1}{1 + e^{-x}} \quad s$$

This is also called the logistic curve, or more commonly the 'S' shaped curve.

Figure 18   The Total Product Curve with the accompanying Marginal Product and Average Product curves

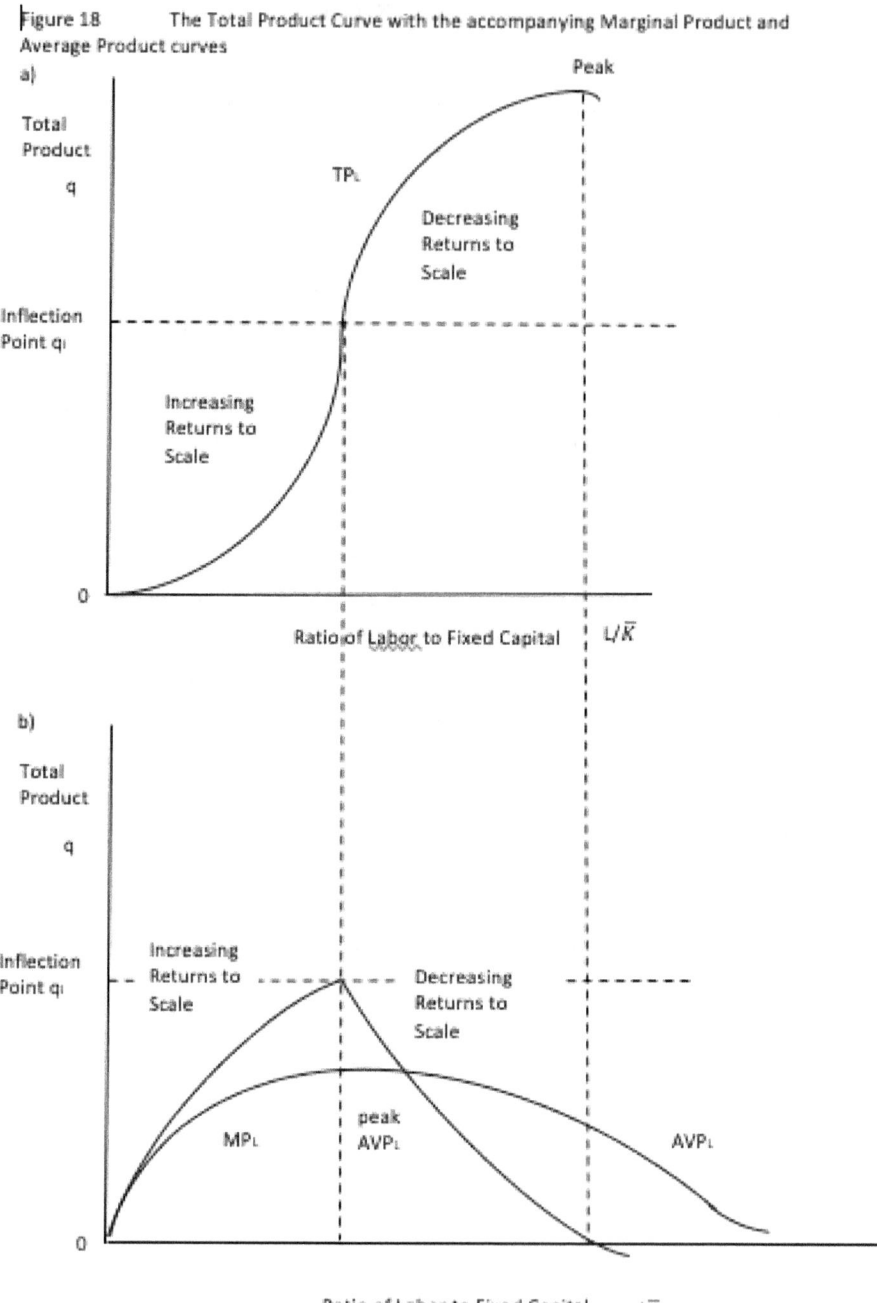

a)

Total Product q

Inflection Point q_I

Peak

TP_L

Decreasing Returns to Scale

Increasing Returns to Scale

Ratio of Labor to Fixed Capital $L/\bar{K}$

b)

Total Product q

Inflection Point q_I

Increasing Returns to Scale

Decreasing Returns to Scale

MP_L

peak AVP_L

AVP_L

Ratio of Labor to Fixed Capital $L/\bar{K}$

The first part of the curve from 0 to *a* is concave downwards. The inflection point *a* has no value.

The second part of the curve from a onwards is concave upwards.

However, the top of the product curve in Figure 18 is flat. That implies that in Figure 19, the marginal product at this point is zero. So, the curve from a must come down, and cross the L/K line at *b* when q = 0.

The marginal product curve crosses the average product curve at its peak, when the slope of the average product curve is zero.

It might be useful at this point to supply four standard diagrams for the production side of microeconomics. These are in Figure 19 below, diagrams (a), (b), (c) and (d).

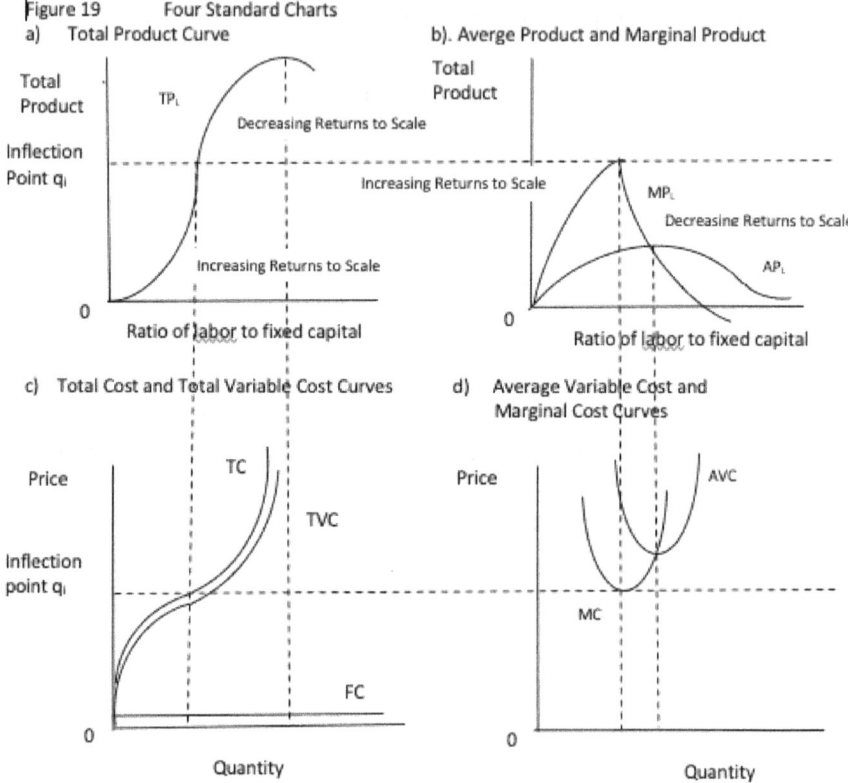

Figure 19   Four Standard Charts

a)   Total Product Curve

b). Averge Product and Marginal Product

c)   Total Cost and Total Variable Cost Curves

d)   Average Variable Cost and Marginal Cost Curves

Figure 19, Chart (a) shows the Sigmoid shape of the growth of Total Product.

Chart (b) shows the marginal product and average product curves derived from the total product curve. The first part of the marginal product curve is concave down, and thus is increasing returns to scale. The second part of the marginal product curve from the inflection point onwards is concave up and decreasing returns to scale. Dividing the total product by total labor gives the curved average product curve passes through the peak of the average product curve., rising to a peak but never falling to zero.

This average product curve with the denominator being labor is the measure of labor productivity, which reaches a peak and then declines. It is interesting to note that while the firm continues to operate under increasing returns to scale labor productivity can never decline. Declining labor productivity is a sign of declining returns to scale.

Chart (c) introduces costs, which are divided into two parts, fixed costs and variable cost. Total fixed costs is the flat line a the bottom. Total variable costs is the curved line rising from zero, and its shape reflects the total product curve at the top. Total costs are the total variable costs plus unit fixed costs, so it parallels the total variable cost line.

Chart (d) demonstrates the relationship between Marginal Cost and Marginal Product, when you add costs from Chart (c) to marginal product and average product. The curves now go in the opposite directions. Marginal cost turns upwards at the inflection point and passes through minimum average variable cost.

As is shown, $MC = \dfrac{\$W}{MP}$

$AVC = \dfrac{\$W}{AP}$

Where $\$W$ is the monetary value of wages (it could be any unit cost).

Thus, there is a direct relationship between marginal product and marginal cost

CHAPTER NINE

THE DOWNWARD SLOPING REVERSE TICK SUPPLY CURVE

Introducing the relationship with marginal revenue

The relationship between marginal revenue and marginal cost is shown in Figure 20.

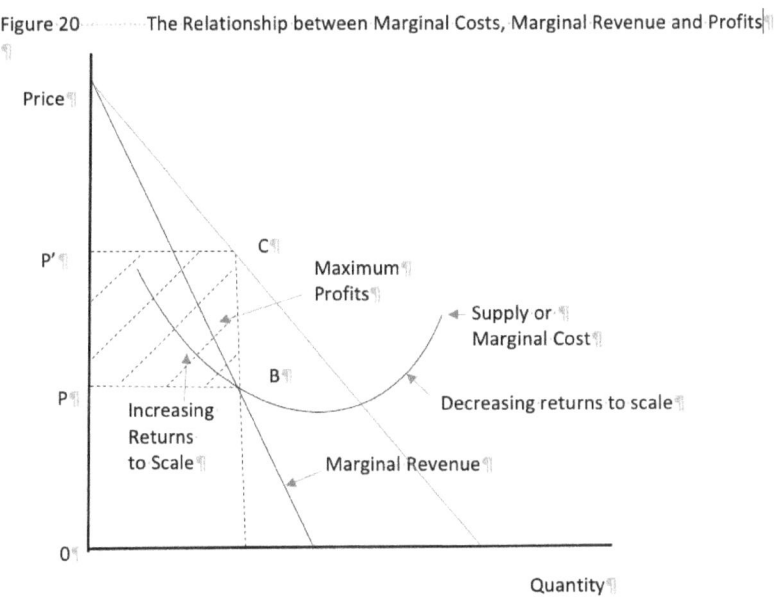

Figure 20 ·········· The Relationship between Marginal Costs, Marginal Revenue and Profits

Maximum Total Profit is the are PP'CB where B is where MR = MC. Where MC crosses the AR line, P – P' = 0, and as profit is P – P' x Q, profit is zero.

The component of the Supply Curve that is profitable is that part of the Supply Curve that is under the Average Revenue curve. The Supply Curve/Marginal Cost curve ceases to exist above the Average Revenue curve. The reason is that there is no profit to be made supplying goods above the Average Revenue curve, as zero profits are made at this point. Thus, there is no point supplying goods when Marginal Costs exceed Average Revenue as the firm would make a loss.

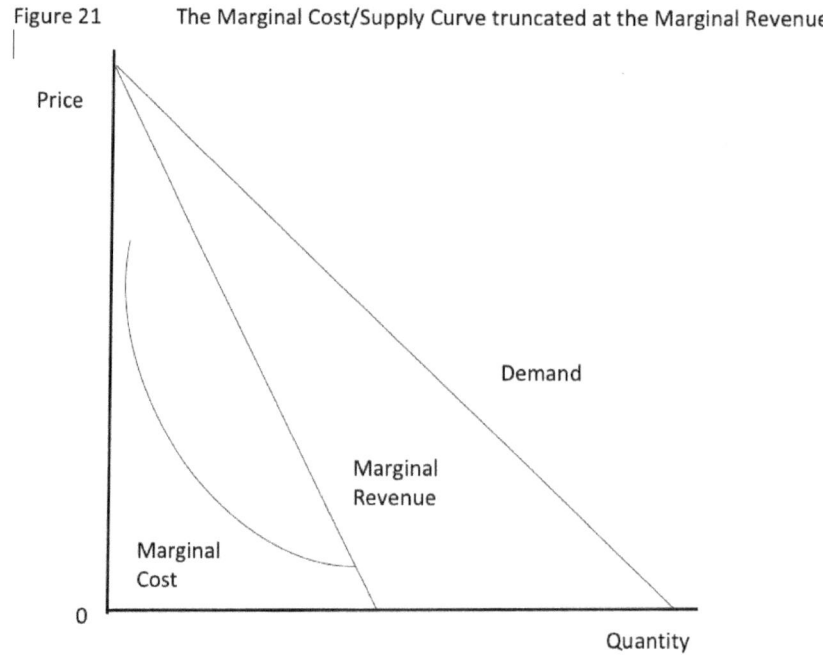

Figure 21   The Marginal Cost/Supply Curve truncated at the Marginal Revenue Curve

An immediate conclusion from Figure 21 is that the Decreasing Returns to Scale component of the Marginal Cost line is likely to be shorter than the Increasing Returns to Scale component. This has and important implication for the forthcoming chapters.

In economic usage the Marginal cost curve is equivalent to the Supply curve. The proof for this statement is in Appendix 1.The Supply Curve describes to schedule of prices that a firm can supply its product at various quantities. The reason for this relationship is that as a firm's output changes, its cost per unit of output can change. The change in the cost per unit is called the marginal cost. At any level output, the minimum price a firm can supply an extra unit of product is at the marginal cost. The marginal cost schedules are called the firm's supply curve.

Comparative lengths of Supply and Demand Lines

A straight-line diagram of Figure 21 would look like Figure 22. Figure 22 makes the concept clearer. What it makes clear is that the Decreasing Returns to Scale Marginal Cost line/Supply line is shorter than the Increasing Returns to Scale Marginal Cost line/Supply line. This has important implications for the forthcoming chapters.

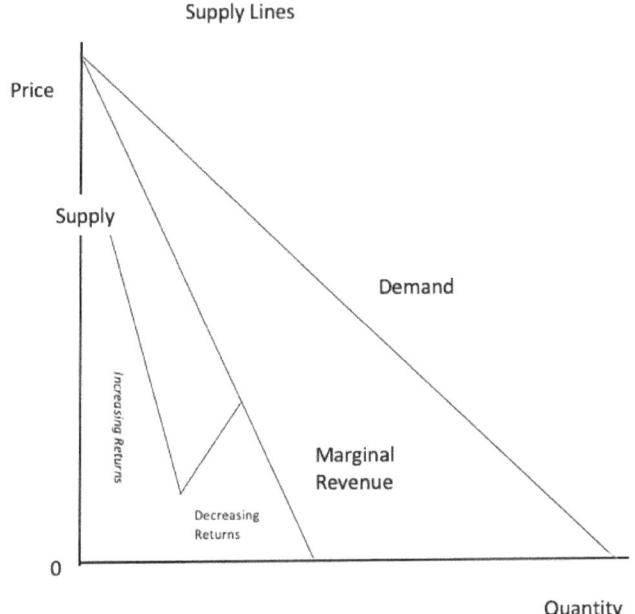

Figure 22   The Comparative Lengths of the Increasing and Decreasing Returns Supply Lines

In the following Figure 23, if you eliminate the Demand and Marginal Revenue lines in Figure 22, you are left with a diagram of the revised Supply lines, showing the downward sloping Increasing Returns supply line contacting the upward sloping Decreasing Returns supply line.

The revised line looks like a line with an "up-tick" at the end. Completely different from the frequently shown upward sloping Supply Line crossing a downward sloping Demand line, as in Figure 1.

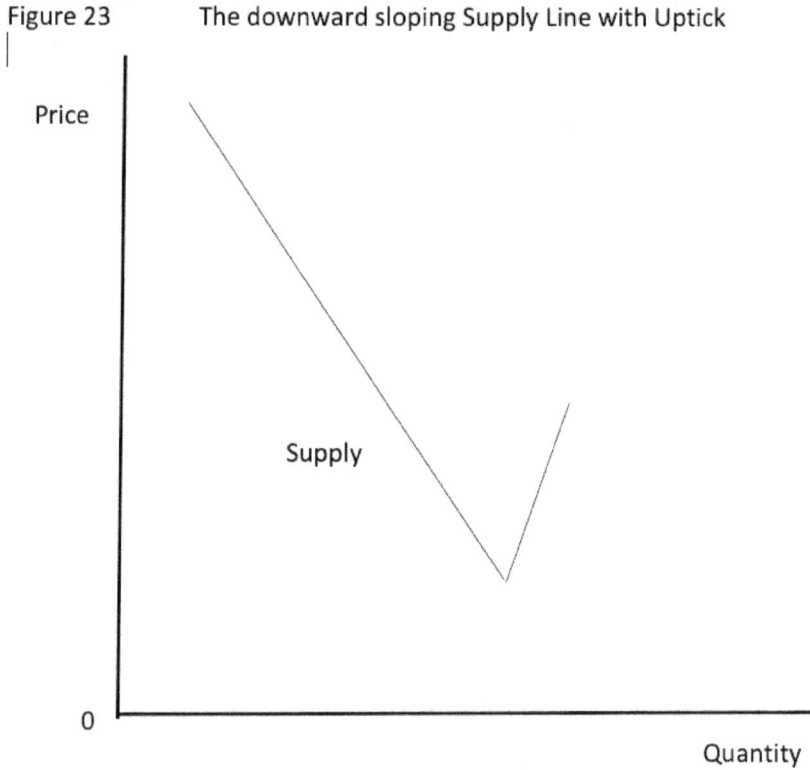

Figure 23   The downward sloping Supply Line with Uptick

Price

Supply

0

Quantity

Note that the decreasing returns to scale supply lines is truncated at the average revenue line. This is because when the

50

Supply (Marginal cost) line meets the Marginal Revenue line, profits are zero, and thus it would not pay the firm to supply further goods or services.

The immediate conclusion is that the decreasing returns to scale line is invariably shorter than the increasing returns to scale line.

While the firm increases it profits while it is operating under increasing returns to scale, the longer the firm delay profit maximising while ceasing to enter decreasing returns to scale the greater is its potential expansion. Decreasing returns to scale effectively places a limit on future expansion.

In other words, profit maximisation is not necessarily the main aim of the firm. A rational firm would preer to expand as far as possible first.

Multiple Equilibria

On a slightly separate issue, Paul Romer said that among his results "multiple equilibria" are possible with an increasing returns to scale supply curve.

If you look at Figure 24, you can see that this is possible if the marginal cost/ supply curve is close to the marginal revenue curve and weaves in and out. This is allowed by a downward sloping supply curve.

An upward sloping supply curve can only have a simple equilibrium value.

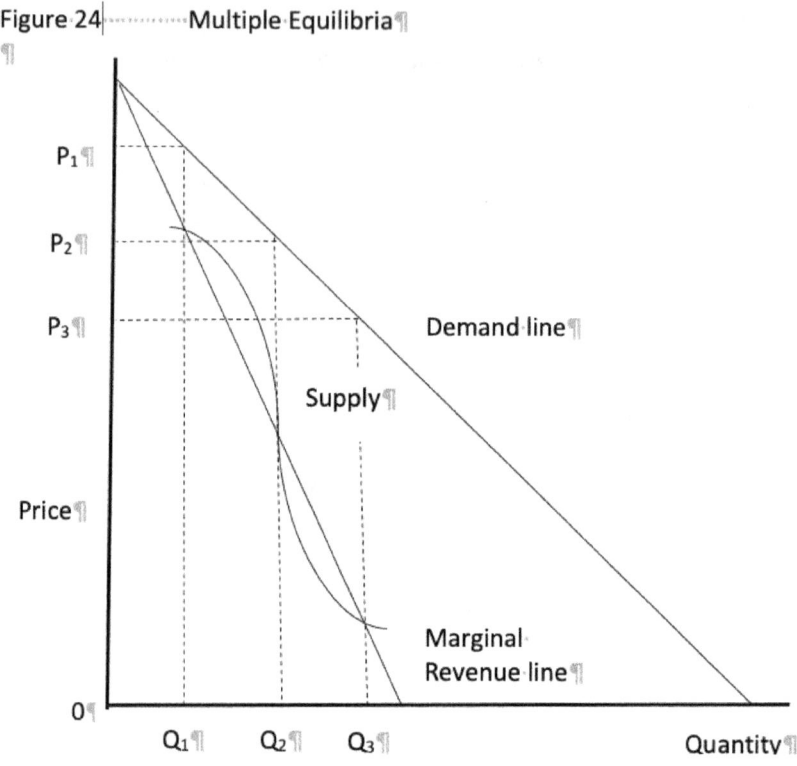

Figure 24   Multiple Equilibria

P₁

P₂

P₃   Demand line

Supply

Price

Marginal
Revenue line

0

Q₁   Q₂   Q₃   Quantity

CHAPTER TEN

THE IMPLICATIONS FOR COMPANY GOVERNANCE OF INCREASING AND DECREASING RETURNS TO SCALE

Figure 25 shows the supply and marginal revenue for a single firm.

Figure 25 Implications for Company Governance of Increasing and Decreasing Returns to Scale

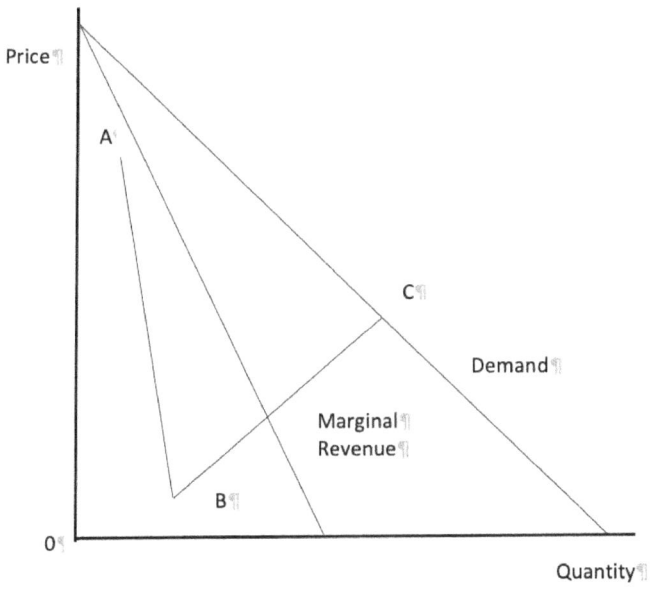

As can be seen in the above figure, the increasing returns to scale curve declines from A to B, and the decreasing returns to scale curve goes upwards from B to C, at the demand curve, where it ceases as the firm ceases to be profitable. A firm

operating under increasing returns to scale continues to make profits as it is operating under the marginal revenue curve. It continues to expand indefinitely until it suddenly starts operating under decreasing returns to scale. Then expansion slows down.

There is usually no constant returns to scale. Where increasing returns to scale meets decreasing returns to scale at B, there is usually no flat line. The firm suddenly switches from increasing returns to scale to decreasing returns to scale. In a later Chapter I have described empirical analysis that shows that exact constant return to scale does not exist.

It can be asked if a firm can start operating under decreasing returns to scale and never operate under increasing returns to scale. In such a case, expansion is minimal, as the decreasing returns to scale line hits the demand curve after with minimal expansion, and then ceases to make profits. Such a situation is common for small scale firms such as many retailers. Their opportunities for expansion are minimal.

What happens if a firm commences operating under increasing returns to scale, hits B, and then moves along the decreasing returns to scale line to C, where it ceases to make a profit?

At this point, I will say from my own investigations, described in my book *Increasing Returns to Scale*, over half the companies quoted on the Stock Exchanges operate in this nether region, line B to C, between ceased expansion and loss.

It is interesting to note that the standard response by accountants and consultants such as McKinsey is that when the company makes a loss, the company is forced to cut expenses, usually the number of employees. The explanation is that the company then "increases margin" and thus profits. Sometimes this works, sometimes it does not. The reason can be found by glancing at Figure 25, Line BC. The real purpose of a firm reducing costs is to attempt to bring it back to the area of increasing returns. Increasing margins is irrelevant.

Quite often, as my analysis shows in my book *Increasing Returns to Scale*, the reason why the firm is operating under decreasing returns to scale is that it overexpanded its capital stock which is now inefficient, not overexpanded its labor force. If the firm's labor force is efficient, reducing the labor force is the wrong factor to reduce. After the exercise of reducing labor, regardless of increased margins, the firm is still operating under decreasing returns to scale and is no better off.

In other words, mere "cost cutting" is not necessarily the best policy. The firm's management must know what they are doing. If the firm is making a loss, it <u>must</u> be operating under decreasing returns to scale. The management must then ask, is either or both factors of production, labor or capital, inefficient. It must then aim to return to increasing returns to scale by either:

1. Increasing sales by the necessary amount
2. Reducing the inefficient factor of production, capital and/or labor, by the necessary amount.

Again, I stress reading my book *Increasing Returns to Scale*, as the methodology described is a far more useful exercise than using the trite accounting solutions of "reducing costs".

CHAPTER ELEVEN

RECENT DEVELOPMENTS IN THE THEORY OF INCREASING RETURNS TO SCALE

As previously discussed, the theory or use of the concept of increasing returns to scale died soon after Adam Smith's first chapter of *Wealth of Nations*. Malthus, and then Ricardo, secured the immutable place of constant returns to scale in economic discourse. If you were a Marxist or a socialist, and all their successors in the field of economics, you had to believe in constant returns to scale, also possibly decreasing returns to scale, but denigrate the concept of increasing returns to scale.

Alfred Marshall (Marshall 1899) briefly raised the question of increasing returns to scale, but said that this was due to exogenous causes. And so that was believed from then on. The major academic subjects of Walrasian General Equilibrium, Leontief Input-Output, and various Critiques by Sraffa, etc just reinforced the requirements for constant returns to scale. To question this in economics was not only decried; if you were in academia it threatened your job!

Alleyn Young (Young 1928) briefly raise a complaint that increasing returns to scale was not looked at, but his paper was largely ignored.

Again, the investigation of the concept of increasing returns to scale largely died for nearly 60 years until Paul Romer became interested in the subject in about 1980. Increasing Returns to Sale became a giant blank spot in economics. Economic theory was based on constant returns to scale and decreasing returns to scale. Increasing returns to scale did not exist.

CHAPTER TWELVE

ROMER'S MODEL OF ENDOGENOUS GROWTH THROUGH INCREASING RETURNS TO SCALE

Increasing returns to scale needed a trail-blazer, indeed an ice-breaker, that broke the pack ice of constant returns to scale, and led to the open waters of increasing returns to scale. Such a person was Paul Romer. If you look at Paul Romer's career, he moved from university to university. He never was in one place for more than a couple of years. Whether he was restless, or the moves were due to antagonism he felt from fellow academics, you will have to ask him. Yet starting in 1983, he continued to publish on the subject of increasing returns to scale. Romer (1983), Romer (1986), Romer (1987). It was not until Romer (1990), the paper called "Endogenous Technological Change", Journal of Political Economy, 98, S71-S102, was Romer generally recognised that he had produce something major. Jones (2019) stated that this was the "most important paper in the growth literature since Solow's Nobel recognise work." For this pathbreaking work Romer was accorded the Nobel Prize in 2018.

So, what was the novel insight in Romer's 1990 paper? It was not that he was just talking about increasing returns to scale. He had been doing that for years. But he nailed the concept of increasing returns to scale with continuous growth in the economy, by introducing the concept of the non-rival characteristic of ideas. Unlike physical resources, such as commodities and labour, that are rival goods, ideas are nonrival.

Rival goods are goods that have to be apportioned among the users. If one user has partial or total use of this good, then another user cannot use that part of the good that is already being used.

Nonrival goods are goods that can be simultaneously used by everyone. If one person is or has used this good, this does not reduce the use for everyone else. An example of a nonrival good is an idea. For example, if one person uses the Pythagorean Theorem, it does not reduce the ability of everyone else to use this Theorem.

An example given by Romer was the recently discovered cure for diarrhea, oral rehydration therapy. By just dissolving a few inexpensive minerals, salts and sugars in water in the right proportions produces a solution that rehydrates children and saves their lives. Once this idea was discovered it could be used to save the lives of countless children time and again.

But once you have increasing returns, output per person depends on the total stock of knowledge – a nonrival good. By implication, there are no physical limits to growth. There are no "Limits to Growth" due to constraints on resources, which was the panic in the 1980's. As Romer points out, in the United States, growth continues at 2 per cent per annum exponentially, and has for centuries, regardless. Long run growth is determined endogenously, which means that the economy produces more knowledge, which in turn produces more growth. Romer briefly discusses the possibility that people will one day run out of ideas, and that will reduce growth, but he cannot give a reason for that happening.

One theoretical result of Romer's increasing returns breakthrough is that increasing returns associated with nonrivalry means that a perfect equilibrium with no externalities does not exist. This result has a fundamental effect on the teaching of fundamental economics for students. Sooner or later, all those textbooks will have to be revised in a major way. See T.J. Kehoe, D.K. Levine, P.M. Romer (1992), "On characterising the equilibrium of economics with externalities and taxes as solutions to the optimisation problem", Economic Theory, pp. 43-68.

In other words, increasing returns to scale can also lead to the concept of multiple equilibria. Not the single equilibrium loved by promoters of pure competition. This result has major implications for macroeconomic policy. In an economy, multiple equilibria can exist, as the economy could, even would, be operating under increasing returns to scale, otherwise it would not be growing. Thus, if an economy is at one equilibrium it can be "jumped" to another equilibrium.

Keynes was instinctively correct on this point, but he could only describe his ideas in words. His opinions had no theoretical basis at the time.

Even though Romer in his Nobel Prize speech was very circumspect and did not mention multiple equilibria, in retrospect the multiple equilibria result will have a more far reaching influence than the somewhat theoretical endogenous growth theory. It will rapidly become a centrepiece of macroeconomic policy

But overall, Romer will be revered for his quiet persistence. He kept plugging away at his attempt to bring back the concept of increasing returns to scale to the centre stage of both economic theory and economic policy. For that, in the years to come, the world will be thankful.

Romer's model

The following is Romer's 1990 (Romer 1990) model, that is the basis of his further developments of the increasing returns to sale model.

We won't discuss the first two parts of Romer's paper, as they just form the introduction of his concept of knowledge as a non-rival good. In Part III he states that his model has four inputs, capital, labour, human capital, and an index of the level of technology. Furthermore, he separates the rival component of knowledge, H, from the non-rival component technological component, A. A can grow without bound.

The formal model has three sectors. The research sector uses human capital and the existing stock of knowledge to produce new knowledge. An intermediate goods sector uses the designs from the research sector together with foregone output to the producer durables that are available to produce the producer durables that are available for use in final goods production. The final-goods sector uses labor, human capital, and the set of producer durables that are available to produce final output. Output can be either consumed or saved as new capital.

Romer keeps the population and the supply of labor constant, the stock of human capital is fixed and that fraction supplied to the market is also fixed. Thus, the supply of the factors L (Labor), and H (knowledge) fixed. Final output Y is expressed as a function of Labor L, human capital devoted to final output H_y, and physical capital, indexed by an integer i.

I shall use a summary of all Romer's papers in Jones (2019) as it gives a clearer description of Romer's work.

As Jones says, the watershed contribution highlighted by the Nobel Prize Committee in Romer (1990a) makes three key contributions:

1. It identifies none-rivalry of ideas as crucial to econ0mic growth.
2. It highlights the role of profit-maximizing entrepreneurs and imperfect competition.
3. It places the key AK linearity in the production function.

The so-called AK model goes back a long way. A is an exogenous and constant productivity parameter and K is physical capital, but in Romer (1986) K was interpreted as knowledge, and in Lucas (1988) it was replaced by human capital.

In its simplest form, the AK model can be expressed as

$$Y_t = AK_t \qquad (1)$$

and

$$\dot{K_t} = sY_t - \partial K_t. \quad (2)$$

Putting these equations together

$$\frac{\dot{Y_t}}{Y_t} = sA - \partial \quad (3)$$

The growth of the economy is endogenously determined by the fundamental parameters of the economic environment.

As Jones said, the AK insight (i.e., a linear differential equation of the form $\dot{K_t} = sAK_t$ could generate an endogenous exponential growth rate) was the theoretical spark that lit a thousand lamps.

The insight that non-rivalry of ideas is crucial to economic growth led to a deep, intuitive understanding of the cause of economic growth. Instead of dividing the world into capital and labour, Romer made a more basic distinction between non-rival ideas and everything else (call them "objects"). Objects were traditional goods that appear in economics, including capital, labor, human capital, land etc. An idea is a design, a blueprint, a set of instructions used to generate more output.

Objects are *rival*; designs are *non-rival*.

From this, Romer demonstrated mathematically that nonrivalry of ideas means that production is characterised by increasing returns to scale.

Romer's basic production function (Romer 1990a) is:

$$Y = F(A, X). \qquad (1)$$

Given a certain quantity of objects X and the set of knowledge A, the function F(·) gives the quantity of output.

Now consider the properties of F(·). If you multiply the number of objects of X by γ, where $\gamma > 1$, then

$$F(A, \gamma X) = \gamma Y \qquad (2)$$

This is constant returns to scale. However, if you multiply the nonrival factor A by γ also:

$$F(\gamma A, \gamma X) > F(A, \gamma X) \qquad (3)$$

That is, production is characterised by *increasing returns to scale*.

Each idea need be only invented once, and then it is technologically feasible for the idea to be used by any number of people or firms simultaneously and repeatedly.

Now how does increasing returns leads to sustained exponential growth?

With increasing returns, you no longer pay all inputs at their marginal product. This outcome, after over a hundred years of usage and assumptions, upsets economists. Romer (1990a) imported the concept of imperfect competition. The key to making these models applicable was the recognition that ideas, while nonrival, are no pure public goods.

Using this insight, the decentralised allocation in the Romer model features entrepreneurial researchers who hunt for new ideas because of the financial rewards that can be earned by innovating. Romer says that innovators are awarded a patent (I say the mere fact of increasing returns to scale) allows them to charge a mark-up over the marginal cost.

A third contribution of Romer (1990a) was to put the AK structure in the idea of the production function. Romer follows the notation that the stock of stock of knowledge is A, and reserving K for physical capital.

With A_t as the stock of ideas at date t, the flow of new ideas is denoted

$$\dot{A}_t = \theta H_{At} A_t \qquad (4)$$

where H_{At} is the amount of human capital devoted to research $\theta > 0$ is a parameter governing the productivity of research. There are increasing returns to H_A and A in this idea of the production function. New ideas lead to positive knowledge spill overs that raise the productivity of future researchers.

The economy is endowed with constant units of human capital that can be used to produce either consumption goods or ideas. Letting $s_t = H_{At}/\bar{H}$ be the fraction of the stock of human capital that is devoted to research, we can rewrite equation (4) as

$$\frac{\dot{A}_t}{A_t} = \theta s_t \bar{H} \qquad (5)$$

Profits incentivise people to search for new ideas. Equation (5) pins down the long-term growth rate of the economy.

In this way, the three key ingredients – the nonrivalry of ideas, the profit motive of imperfect competition (caused by increasing returns to scale), and putting the key linear differential equations in the production function – combine to generate the insight of Romer (1990a).

The non-rivalry of ideas makes sustained exponential growth possible. Romer was the first to truly understand the implications of non-rivalry – and the increasing returns it implies - for economic growth.

CHAPTER THIRTEEN

ADDING THE ENTERPRISE QUOTIENT TO ROMER'S MODEL

The next chapter discusses of Paul Romer's (Romer 1990a) model, previous described. While this model is very effective in describing the relationship between knowledge, increasing returns to scale and growth, there was something missing. What was missing was motivated actions. Why was knowledge so readily converted into growth? Another question was that this model, like so many others, was U.S. centric. Why, if roughly the same amount of knowledge was readily available throughout the world, why was growth so different? The excuse that there were different levels of education in different countries was vague. Firms in these countries could still use the universal knowledge base regardless.

I propose inserting an additional variable into Romer's equations, the Enterprise Quotient, or E. This describes the amount of 'push' in each country to adapt new knowledge to business activity, and harness it to growth; or alternatively the 'spirit' of enterprise in each country. Those countries that have a low Enterprise Quotient would have a low rate of growth, while those that had a high level of Enterprise Quotient would have a high rate of growth.

Adapting Romer's (Romer 1990a) model

Referring back Chapter Twelve, in Romer (1990a), Romer's basic production function was

$$Y = F(A, X) \tag{1}$$

Now we change Romer's model slightly. Growth Y is also dependent on the product of the Entrepreneurial Push, or Enterprise, amount E, times A, the amount of knowledge.

This is because knowledge itself is inactive. It has to be used. Assuming that "exists and therefore it is used" is incorrect. There has to someone who is motivated to use the knowledge, and will actively use it. It is not enough to say that there is a profit incentive. There has to be someone who actively brings knowledge and the profit incentive together. There has to be an Entrepreneurial Push. I call this Enterprise.

So Romer's initial model is changed by including the Enterprise, E

$$Y = F(EA, X) \tag{1a}$$

Then equation (2) is modified to

$$F(EA, \gamma X) = \gamma Y \tag{2a}$$

Then equation (3) is modified to

$$F(E\gamma A, \gamma X) > F(EA, \gamma X) \tag{3a}$$

Again, the production that includes these activities of the Entrepreneur is operating under increasing returns to scale.

The flow of new ideas is now denoted by
$$\dot{A}_t = \theta H_{At} E A_t \tag{4a}$$

Entrepreneurial influence increases the flow of new ideas.

We can rewrite (4a) as

$$\frac{\dot{A}_t}{A_t} = \theta s_t \overline{H} E \qquad (5a)$$

The long - term growth of the economy is increased by the product of E, the level of Enterprise, in the economy.

I call E the Enterprise Quotient E.Q.

It can be seen that the explanation that growth rates vary between different regions is because of the different amounts of entrepreneurial influence between regions. Romer's model assumes that the quantity of knowledge A is equally available between different regions, and does not have an explanation to why it is not.

Quite simply the different influence of entrepreneurs between regions has been discussed by economic historians for generations. There are two major factors – the actual number of entrepreneurs differ, and the social and historical influences encouraging entrepreneurial action differ greatly between regions.

CHAPTER FOURTEEN

ESTIMATING INCREASING RETURNS TO SCALE

Many people, at least economist supporters of constant returns to scale, may continue to claim that in the real world, most firms operate under constant or decreasing returns to scale. They have no evidence for this belief, but it continues to be an article of faith. This attitude stems from their training, and also from their frequent left-wing values. They say "Whatever theory says, common sense says that the vast majority of firms operate under constant or decreasing returns to scale."

I am willing to concede that non-profit making institutions, such as government bureaucracies, are highly inefficient and operate under decreasing returns to scale; but profit-making entities must of necessity operate under increasing returns to scale, or for a limited period under decreasing returns to scale. Since constant returns to scale has been shown to not exist (see Chapter Two) they cannot operate under constant returns to scale.

Do I have any evidence of this?

I refer to my book *Increasing Returns to Scale: A Simple Way to Make Good Investments and not Bad Investments when Investing in Company Shares*. Not a bad read. For those who want to increase the value of their investment or retirement fund, a necessity. Depending on how well the method described in the book is used, the gains are in the double-digit percentages over some index such as the Dow, as increasing return companies almost invariably increase in value. The converse is not necessarily true, at least for long periods. The market is not totally rational.

The book is a "how-to-do" book, and so, for the purpose of this chapter does not provide a complete list of all companies due to lack of space. I have found from my experience that about half the largest top 500 firms operate under increasing returns to scale. Among smaller firms, the proportion is much higher. As a rule of the thumb, as the firm increases in size, the likelihood of the firm operating under increasing returns to scale decreases. My inference is, nearly all un-quoted small firms operate under increasing returns to scale. Since my book was aimed at investing in firms quoted on the stock exchange, I have no evidence to support this inference. But since Romer's conclusion is that the macro-economy operates under increasing returns to scale, I have no reason to doubt my conclusion that most firms, and the vast bulk of the economy, operates under increasing returns to scale.

So how does this method work?

The methodology depends on the Cobb-Douglas Production function.

$$Y = DK^\alpha L^\beta$$

Where
Y = the firm's revenue in that year
K = the firm's value of capital in that year
L = the firm's labor cost in that year
D is a fixed coefficient
α = the relative efficiency of capital of the firm
β = the relative efficiency of labor of the firm

$\alpha + \beta$ = the measure of returns to scale

If $\alpha > 0$ the revenue elasticity of expenditure for capital expenditure is positive. This means that for every additional dollar invested in capital, revenue increases by the same amount of dollars.

If $\alpha < 0$ the revenue elasticity of expenditure for capital expenditure is negative. This means that for every additional dollar invested capital, revenue decreases by the same amount of dollars.

If $\beta > 0$ the revenue elasticity of expenditure for labor expenditure is positive. This means that for every additional dollar invested spent on labor, revenue increases by the same amount of dollars.

If $\beta < 0$ the revenue elasticity of expenditure for labor expenditure is negative. This means that for every additional dollar spent on labor, revenue decreases by the same amount of dollars.

Data is extracted for two successive years, marked 1 and 2.

The above two functions 1 and 2 are then logged.

Assuming α and β are unchanged over the two following years, then:

$$\beta = \frac{\ln Y_1 - \alpha \ln k_1}{\ln L_1}$$

or

$$\beta = \frac{\ln Y_2 - \alpha \ln k_2}{\ln L_2}$$

$$\alpha = \frac{\ln L_2 \ln Y_1 - \ln L_1 \ln Y_2}{\ln L_2 \ln K_1 - \ln L_1 \ln K_2}$$

α is the relative efficiency of capital expenditure

β is the relative efficiency of labor

L is the quantity of labor, K is the quantity of capital, and Y is income in the respective periods 1 and 2.

Data. For the US, I used the SEC 10-K site for financial data. Dry but informative. Company Annual Reports are difficult to use, and often try to hide important information.

I tested using statistical regression whether $\alpha_1 = \alpha_2$ and $\beta_1 = \beta_2$. I found that they equalled within a 95% confidence interval.

In conclusion, using this empirical method, I have found that around half the large quoted firms in the USA operated under increasing returns to scale, and a much higher proportion of smaller quoted firms operated under increasing returns to scale. My untested inference is that nearly all small un-quoted firms above the size of "small business" operate under increasing returns to scale. That would be an objective for a very important empirical investigation.

The attached is a snippet from my book "*Increasing Returns to Scale*". This table gives a calculated measure of increasing and decreasing returns to scale for selected companies in the year 2013. I might add that many have profited from using this simple technique.

Alpha is the returns to scale for capital, and beta is the returns to scale for labor. Added together, they are the total returns to scale for the company. If the individual amounts or the total are above one, then that means increasing returns to scale for that variable. If the amount is less than one, that means decreasing returns to scale for that variable. This table was for the year

2013. Things could have changed since then, so I don't advise using the table to make investment. I suggest that you buy the book and use it to make your own calculations.

Table 1 Estimation of Increasing and Decreasing Returns to Scale for selected companies

Company name	Y1 Income Year1	K1 Capital Year 1	L1 Wages Year 1	Y2 Income Year 2	K2 Capital Year 2	L2 Wages Year 2	α	B	$\alpha+\beta$ Returns to Scale
American Express	33776	153140	6597	34932	153375	6171	1.22	-0.47601	0.7480093
Apple	65225	75183	7299	108249	116371	10028	3.08	-2.64341	0.4382604
BP	375765	146323	12327	379136	151457	13117	1.72	-0.81277	0.9102306
Caterpillar	2693	34742	416	2783	35138	427	0.03	1.242839	1.2841405
Chevron	253706	209474	26394	241909	232982	27294	-1.34	2.837582	1.4953760
Coca Cola	46542	79974	28327	48017	86174	28964	0.15	0.875391	1.029533
Disney	36149	63117	30452	38063	69206	31337	0.36	0.624993	0.990787
Du Pont	36144	51499	29142	35310	49859	32252	0.91	0.0602924	0.9705306
General Electric	147288	718189	54185	147359	685328	53912	-0.14	1.274510	1.126768
General Motors	150276	144603	130386	152256	149422	140236	1.48	-0.49091	0.998962
IBM	127245	116433	55533	104507	119213	53122	0.95	0.035215	0.994924
Intel	53999	71119	36262	53441	84351	28395	0.56	0.441307	1.001957
JP Morgan Chase	97031	2359141	30585	96606	2415689	30810	0.72	0.085639	0.806392
Microsoft	73723	121271	38237	77849	142431	30836	0.70	0.274599	0.984502
Pepsi	66504	72882	31593	65492	74638	31291	-0.14	1.231123	1.083732
Shell	470171	345257	14335	467153	360325	14616	-1.95	3.968702	2.014392

CHAPTER FIFTEEN

CONSEQUENCES FOR THEORIES THAT RELY ON CONSTANT RETURNS TO SCALE

As has already been noted, constant returns to scale does not exist. The increasing returns to scale supply curve meets the decreasing returns to scale supply curve with no or minimal intermediary constant returns to scale.

The concept of constant returns to scale has been a fundamental component of economics going back two hundred years. The concept of constant returns to scale provides a foundation of economic theory from Ricardo through Marxism to General Equilibrium to Input Output Theory. Without this fundamental assumption of constant returns to scale, a whole slew of academic economics ceases to exist. No constant returns to scale, no whatever it depends on.

Consequences for Marxism

Marxism assumes constant returns to scale in its labor theory of value, derived from David Ricardo's labor theory of value. No constant returns to scale. No labor theory of value. Simple. Then no exploitation.

Marxism is also heavily dependent on the concept of decreasing returns to scale to predict the doom of capitalism. A small truncated length, compared to the much larger length of the increasing returns to scale schedule, seems to imply perpetual growth for the capitalist system!

Consequences for Walrasian General Equilibrium

As already been mentioned, Walrasian General Equilibrium not only depends on non-existent constant returns to scale, but also depends on an un-restricted length of a decreasing returns to scale curve. The short length decreasing returns to scale supply line has serious repercussions for Walrasian General Equilibrium. Even if a workaround can be found for the non-existence of constant returns to scale, a "cap" on the decreasing returns to scale quantity severely hampers the results.

The results obtained using a G-E model would be highly inaccurate if constant returns to scale is assumed, as it is probable the economy as a whole operates under increasing returns to scale. if an unlimited decreasing returns to scale schedule was assumed, this leads to further inaccurate results.

Can the General Equilibrium model be rescued by switching solely to an increasing returns to scale schedule? That is an interesting question.

Consequences for Input-Output Theory

The Leontief Input-Output theory depends fundamentally on the existence of constant returns to scale. At one time, with the onset of computers, the Input-Output process was very popular among management consultants. It has since fallen out of favour, as the results clearly were nonsense. However, input-output theory survives in some nooks of academia.

Consequence for the standard textbook diagram

Finally, the standard textbook description of a supply curve should be changed. Instead of the upward sloping supply line crossing a downward sloping demand line, as shown in Figure 1, it should be in the form of a reverse tick, as seen in Figure 25, meeting but not crossing the marginal revenue line.

As can be seen, the supply line initially goes downward, underneath the marginal revenue line, operating under increasing returns to scale. Then the supply line ticks upwards, operating for a shorter length under decreasing returns to scale, until it hits the marginal revenue line. And then further supply cannot progress further as it is unprofitable, and the supply line ceases.

PART II

ENTERPRISE AND VENTURE CAPITAL

Before we go onto a description of Enterprise and Venture Capital, there will be those who question why this book commenced and devoted over half the pages to a description of microeconomics? I could have just jumped into a set of vague maxims, and say "just do it.

But a budding Venture Capitalist, I feel, needs a greater understanding of basic economics. Where it all fits in. More than just do what has worked, and everybody does this...!

Now, hopefully, you know what Increasing Returns to Scale means, and why this is the ultimate aim of venture capital. If things go wrong, you will have some theoretical concepts in the back of your mind to guide you back to a safe haven. Don't rely on consultants with their accounting-based advice. Cutting costs only work if the firm is operating under decreasing returns to scale. Check first if you are operating under increasing returns to scale, (using my book "Increasing Returns to Scale"), and if not, how to get back to it.

CHAPTER SIXTEEN

ENTERPRISE

The definitions usually used for Enterprise are vague and not very useful. I shall use a definition that is more operationally useful, as follow:

Definition

"Enterprise is the action to start a firm to produce and sell a good or service, and it is intended that the firm would operate under increasing returns to scale." That is, it is intended that the firm would have employees and would operate with the division of labour.

There is no requirement for the enterprise to be original. Copy. Copy. But just do it better. There are a whole range of entrepreneurs, such as Mark Zuckerberg with Facebook and Elon Musk with electric cars, who were not original, but in some way they got there first, and were highly successful.

A firm starting up as a sole trader, such as a truck driver, would not be under this definition be an entrepreneur, as he would not be creating wealth by the division of labour. Such a person just would be "buying a job", in the words of self-help books, and would not be able to go away for a holiday, and be able to receive an income from his business in his absence.

A useful model using the Enterprise Quotient E I described in Chapter Eight is Romer's adapted model. This is a useful operational definition.

Term (5a) says

$$\frac{\dot{A_t}}{A_t} = \theta s_t \overline{H} E$$

In effect Romer's model says that the long-term growth of the economy is caused by increasing returns to scale. By adding E, long-term growth is given impetus by Enterprise.

As has already been described, the process of wealth creation is tied up in increasing returns to scale. No increasing returns to scale, no profits, or sustainable profits over a long period. And has been seen in Chapter Eight, it is enterprise that places the firm in the zone of increasing returns to scale and thus creates wealth.

Thus Enterprise, Increasing Returns to Scale and wealth creation are ineluctably joined. Yes, you could start a small firm that does not expand as it already operates under decreasing returns to scale, and create a minimal amount of wealth. But to repeat, significant wealth is only created by increasing returns to scale, and it takes Enterprise, through action of the Entrepreneur, to do this.

Nearly all wealth creation (except for the tiny amount created under decreasing returns to scale) has the prime cause of Enterprise, through the action of the Entrepreneur, creating a firm operating under increasing returns to scale. No Enterprise, no Entrepreneur, no wealth creation.

There are many alternative definitions of wealth, such as money, resources, land, population, education and human capital, cumulated stock of research, and many other valuable stocks. But stocks depreciate in value. Every year, unless demand is maintained, the value of these stocks of "wealth" can decline. For wealth to be maintained and increased, the demand for these stocks have to be maintained to maintain wealth. Even for money and gold. The demand for money or gold is not fixed. It can go up or down.

Demand in the economy is maintained or increased by the creation of new wealth. If wealth is not created in this economy, which is a flow, demand is not maintained at its present levels and it fall. If demand falls, prices fall, and the value of wealth stocks decline (even the value of gold).

It is thus necessary to maintain a minimum level of entrepreneurial activity. If this is not done, insufficient new wealth is created. Overall demand falls. Prices falls. The value of wealth stocks decline. All value in the economy is maintained by the flow of wealth creation, which is ultimately dependent on the amount of Enterprise in the economy, which ultimately dependent on the number and activities of the Entrepreneurs in the economy. The more entrepreneurs, the more wealth.

So, what is an Entrepreneur, and what does he do? For that we go to the following chapter.

CHAPTER SEVENTEEN

THE ENTREPRENEUR

Over the years the definitions of the entrepreneur tended to be vague, limited and often contradictory. An improved definition is necessary.

In the previous chapter we described Enterprise. How is the definition of the Entrepreneur connected to this definition? And is not sufficient to say that an Entrepreneur is "enterprising"!

Definition

"An Entrepreneur is a person who takes action to start a firm that will operate under increasing returns to scale to produce and sell goods or services".

It was often assumed from definitions used elsewhere that this Entrepreneur must bring together the necessary resources, and also provide the necessary planning and management; but as can be seen in the next chapters on Venture Capital, these requirements are not necessary all. Many recent Venture Capital inceptions required zero capital input by the entrepreneur, and in many cases their management input was rapidly excluded.

For many years the entrepreneur was defined as a "capitalist", providing the necessary capital and management control. This definition is entirely inaccurate. Entrepreneurs can and often do provide neither capital nor management.

It is noted that an integral component of the above definition is increasing returns to scale. Without increasing returns to scale, the entrepreneur's firm would not create wealth for himself and society. It would rapidly cease to exist. The entrepreneur would become a non-entrepreneur!

What about Venture Capitalists? They have a hand in starting numerous enterprises. Are they "multi-entrepreneurs"? No. A venture capitalist is an entrepreneur when he starts his venture capital firm, but after that all these startups are the product of these venture capital firms. They churn them out like bolts of cloth (the modern venture capital firm such as Y-Combinator really does this). It is an industry, on which the venture capital firms make profits.

Now that we have defined an Entrepreneur, what are the entrepreneur's required characteristics? How can they be described?

For this purpose, we need a list of the characteristics of an entrepreneur in the order of importance. It is of course assumed that the putative entrepreneur should be healthy and active, but not necessarily young. But Ray Croc started McDonalds at the age of 52!

Table 2   In my opinion, the characteristics of an entrepreneur in order of importance are:

1. Courage
2. Desires money
3. Desires independence

4. Motivated and persistent
5. Opportunist
6. Finder and user of innovations
7. Initiator
8. Possibly supplies a small amount of capital, but in the modern venture capital environment, this is no longer necessary
9. Personal honesty
10. Organiser and builder
11. Leader
12. Reacts immediately to change

These characteristics are described as follows.

1. Courage. For an entrepreneur to be a risk-taker he needs personal courage. The entrepreneur needs to take a risk with his lifestyle. This is the original and most usual definition. The entrepreneur needs to risk money, time and other interests with the aim of gaining money and personal satisfaction.

   However, many people take risks all the time. Some gamble, others take risks with their careers, some take physical risks for monetary gain or sheer enjoyment. These are not entrepreneurs.

2. Desires money. Psychological surveys say that the desire for more money is an overwhelming motivator for entrepreneurs. Initially they desire financial security for themselves and their family, and then greater status. However, surveys of successful entrepreneurs show that past a certain point, the desire for more money does not concern them.

3. Desires independence. To be your own boss. Psychological surveys of entrepreneurs show that the desire for independence is an overwhelming desire, after the desire for money, that motivates an entrepreneur to go out on their own. While everybody desires more money, most are happy to continue to take orders. The desire for independence is not so overwhelming that they are willing to take the risk and upset their lives to go out on their own. An additional issue is that the vast majority of beings are social animals, and are unwilling to lose their social connections to, at least initially, work on their own.

4. Motivated, active and persistent. This is a pre-requisite. An entrepreneur needs to be a person who constantly takes action, and does not let things slide. If they let extraneous events take priority, and if the can be pushed around, they will get nowhere. As all self-help books say, persistence is the pre-requisite for success.

5. Opportunist. An entrepreneur, at least initially, must seek new opportunities and take advantage of them. A successful continuing entrepreneur must continue to be an opportunist. Not many have this mindset – constantly looking for new opportunities. An entrepreneur must be an opportunist – and act quickly with courage.

6. Finder and user of innovations. An entrepreneur must be an innovator. The best opportunities for an entrepreneur are in the vast un-tapped universe of novel goods and services, where there is no initial competition so there are monopoly rents and large

profits. True, a successful entrepreneur can still operate in known areas, such as franchises, or for example setting up a department store. Many just copy. But the most successful entrepreneurs are visionaries, innovators and opportunists.

7. Initiator. Not a follower. This is a sub-category of courage. If something perceived to be needed to be done, the entrepreneur is the first to say that it needs to be done and what is to be done, and if necessary does it himself.

8. Supplier of capital – maybe. From the days of Adam Smith it was assumed that an entrepreneur must be a capitalist. Being an entrepreneur and a capitalist was considered synonymous. Not anymore. Nowadays, with the growth of venture capital, the needed financial contribution of entrepreneurs has fallen from very little in the days of Allen Noyce and Steve Jobs in the 1970's to nothing at all. It is rare for venture capitalists nowadays to ask for a financial contribution from the putative entrepreneur. Money is cheap, and investors are desperate to throw their money at anything potentially profitable. Capital is no longer part of the entrepreneurial makeup.

9. Personal honesty. We are now getting down to a basic characteristic of a successful entrepreneur. This should be at the very start, but regrettably a lot of personally dishonest entrepreneurs can create successful start-ups. But after that things go wrong. It is noteworthy that ALL successful venture capitalists look for personal honesty as the PRIME requisite for any entrepreneur they invest in, far above "bankable" ideas. This is from

bitter experience. As one said "We are not paying for excuses, laziness, dishonesty, character defects. They can prove very costly." Most venture capitalists check the CV very carefully.

10. Organiser and builder. At the start the organisation has to be built from scratch. At the start the entrepreneur has to be the sole manager. He has to build a firm that employs people, then divides the roles, which then makes the product and sells it. Not many people, when they have come this far, can change from being a thinker to a doer, and being an organiser.

11. Leader. And yes, that entrepreneur must be a leader. Especially eventually if he has many managers beneath him. He must change again to someone who inspires subordinates to agree with the goals set by the entrepreneur, and actively work towards them.

12. Reacts immediately to change. Change happens. The entrepreneur must rapidly react to change. This is easier said than done. An entrepreneur can get comfortable with his achievements, and become oblivious to the need for change. Maybe the entrepreneur has not set up an efficient communications system, a system that communicates the need for change not only from outside the firm, but also from inside; there must be fast and efficient communication of the need for change from the bottom up. All organizations must change, and change rapidly and be responsive when there is a need for change – or the firm will expire.

The preceding chapter describes the basic requirements of a successful entrepreneur. Many desire to be a successful entrepreneur. Few succeed.

Later on, we describe venture capital. Venture capital has the twin benefits of originating many more entrepreneurial organisations, and helps a much higher proportion to survive and succeed.

CHAPTER EIGHTEEN

THE HISTORY OF THE USE OF THE NAME ENTREPRENEUR

The concept of the entrepreneur has been greatly neglected in economics. Yes, the entrepreneur is occasionally mentioned, but then is sidelined. He is an "economic actor" that automatically does this task of organising, risk taking and providing capital, but his role is take for granted. There are no real consequences for his role. Does the entrepreneur create wealth? Not under constant returns to scale. Under these conditions his role would be exploitive. It would only be the workers that create value, as again, there would be no increasing returns to scale.

The idea that only workers create value is of course derived from the economic theory of Karl Marx. (The labor theory of value). Which in turn depends on the assumption of constant returns to scale. As constant returns to scale in turn does not theoretically exist, as described in this book, we need another source of the creation of wealth. This is the activities of entrepreneurs using increasing returns to scale. Unfortunately, there is not enough room in this book to write a polemic on the theories of Karl Marx. However, it is a basically simple task to contradict his theories, (just go through his theories and delete constant returns to scale), and I shall leave that to the reader. No constant returns to scale, no labor theory of value, no theory of exploitation, and all the rest. Though admittedly Marx never mentioned constant returns to scale. In the primitive economics of the time, that is all that existed, and Marx assumed it was true. Marx relied on the writings of Ricardo and Malthus, and

Adam Smith of course who invented the labor theory of value; and built up from there.

This is not to say workers do not create wealth. But not all of them create wealth. Workers in organisations operating under increasing returns to scale create wealth. Workers in organisations operating under decreasing returns to scale create wealth as long as that organisation is profitable. All the rest of workers, operating under unprofitable decreasing returns to scale and declining returns to scale, consume wealth. They are among that part of society who are consuming and not producing.

If you ask, "What proportion of the wealth created by these workers goes back to them?", in this enquiry we will sidestep the question of distribution (exploitation?). This massive subject in economics has not been resolved. What is a "fair" distribution of the wealth created between the workers and the legal owners of the productive organisation? How is it to be done? Is the proposed re-distribution/wage raising economically efficient? Or to put it another way, which aim is better, the one that maximises the welfare of workers the most? Faster growth or greater re-distribution? Whoever provides a believable solution to this major question will certainly gain a Nobel Prize.

All I would say is that is proportion is set by the market at the time, in proportion to demand and supply for the various resources, including various types of labor.

Indeed, does it matter, if both sides are gaining?

A short history of the use of the term "Entrepreneur"

Discussion of the role and definition of the entrepreneur goes back a long way. The history of the subject has been subject to various cycles of interest and neglect, until in the past thirty years there has been a resurgence of interest. However, this resurgence originated from areas of psychology and business management, not economics. Economic scholarship cannot get a hang of this subject, it seems, and it is still preoccupied with the concepts of equilibrium and pure competition.

Richard Cantillon (in 1725), an early very brilliant monetary economist, who made a fortune selling out early shares in John Law's Mississippi scheme, was the inventor of the term 'entrepreneur', French for undertaker. He defined this person as an agent who takes the risk buys products to combine them into other products. He linked risk, time, organisational ability, and the supplier of capital. His essay "Essai sur la Nature de Commerce en Général" (Cantillon 1725) referred to the "entrepreneur" as a person who bought cheaply at a certain price and sold output at an uncertain price.

Adam Smith (1776) defined an entrepreneur "is a proprietary capitalist, a supplier of capital and at the same time, works as a manager intervening between labour and capital". However, Smith in his foundational Chapter One on the pin factory assumes the factory's existence, and does not discuss the role of the factory's owner and manager. This was the start of a long record of economic thought – assume something was already in place.

Jean Baptiste Say (!803) (of Say's Law "increased supply creates increased demand") goes into further detail. "An entrepreneur is the economic agent who unites all means of production, the land of one, the labour of another and the capital of yet another and thus produces a product. By selling the product in the market, he pays rent of land, wages of labor, interest on capital and what remiss is his profit". Whew! Say thus emphasized the functions of the entrepreneur as co-ordination, organisation and supervision.

Then nothing happens in economics for nearly ninety years. Jeremy Bentham and John Stuart Mill mentioned the entrepreneur in passing, the concept was not central to their attempts at price theory. Economics went down a rabbit hole of the theory of value and distribution, and didn't come up for air until Marshall (1890) crossed supply and demand to obtain price. Yes, economists also discussed utility theory and the elasticity of supply and demand, and got all mathematical with General Equilibrium. But production theory was at a dead end......Constant returns to scale. But Marshall again briefly reintroduced the concept of entrepreneurship as an organiser and coordinator.

The concept of entrepreneur stagnated until in 1921 Frank Knight in his book "Risk, Uncertainty and Profit" argued that the skills of the entrepreneur lay in the in his ability to handle uncertainty. Risk of course was measurable and could be priced.

Again, things died the death until Joseph Schumpeter (1934) assigned for the first time a crucial role of innovator to the entrepreneur in his book "Theory of Economic Development". According to Schumpeter, entrepreneurship is essentially a creative activity. The entrepreneur is the innovator who introduces something new into the economy. He tried to develop an entirely new economic theory based on change, as opposed to equilibrium. He discussed the function of an entrepreneur as an individual who tends to break the equilibrium by introducing innovations into the system,. He argued that "creative destruction is the essential fact of capitalism" and the entrepreneur is the prime agent of economic change.

Hayek (1945) and von Mises (1949) tried to raise the question of entrepreneurship, but nobody listened.

Frederick Harbison in his paper " Entrepreneurial Organisation as a Factor" (1951) placed the entrepreneur at the centre as an organisation builder and leader.

Arthur Cole, an economics professor at Harvard, tried to raise the study of entrepreneurial history through "Journal of Economic History" and his founding of the Harvard Research Center on Economic History, but both died in 1958.

David McClelland, a psychologist, was the first green shoot in the study of entrepreneurial questions in his book "The Achieving Society" (1961). This generated a stream of publications on the subject on the "traits" of individual entrepreneurs.

Baumol (1968) was one of the first economists who tried to re-integrate the entrepreneurial function into economics. He said "There is no room in standard economics for enterprise or initiative. The management group becomes a passive calculation that reacts mechanically to external developments over which it does not exert, and does not even attempt to exert any influence" (p. 67). "The theoretical firm is entrepreneurless – The Prince of Denmark has been expunged from the discussion of Hamlet" (p. 66). The neo-classical model is essentially an instrument of optimality analysis, "maximisation and minimisation have consolidated the foundation of the theory, (but) as a result of this fact the theory is deprived of the ability to possess an analysis of entrepreneurship (p 68).

It was not until Schumpetarian analysis made a comeback in the 1970's in the form of evolutionary economics that the entrepreneur began to make a headway in being incorporated in economic design (Klein 1977) (Nelson and Winter 1982).

From the early 1980's there began an explosion of literature on the subject of entrepreneurs that was connected to the study of small start-ups. However, the study of entrepreneurship remained highly fragmented, with a minimal relationship with economics. The major influences were studies in business management, psychology, social anthropology and finance.

In the past three decades there have been many papers and books written on the subject. Outstanding ones include W. Casson, 1982 "The Entrepreneur: An Economic Theory", PH Brockhaus 1982 "The psychology of an entrepreneur", DC Blanchfloss and AT Oswald, 1988, "What makes an Entrepreneur", DL Sexton and P Kassandra, (Eds), 1992 "The state of the art of entrepreneurships", DC Blanchflower and AJ Oswald 1998, Journal of Labor Economics "What makes an entrepreneur", SJ Parker 2018 "The economics of entrepreneurship". The subject has exploded in recent years, and there are currently at least half a dozen university courses in entrepreneurship.

But the connection with economics remains small. A survey of the literature by Carlson et al (2013) found that economics related papers on entrepreneurship made up of only about two percent of the total. There remained a strong inhibition in the economics profession preventing economists taking an interest in the subject of entrepreneurship.

CHAPTER NINETEEN

VENTURE CAPITAL INVESTING

What is Venture Capital investing? Again, we need a definition.

Definition

"Venture Capital investing is the activity of financing new potentially profitable ventures proposed by un-connected persons with proposals for these ventures".

As can be seen from the above definition, Venture Capital is an investment process, most usually done by a firm, not an individual, that invests in new ventures as a continuing business. The venture capital firm receives business proposals from persons outside the firm, assesses them, and decides whether or not to invest in these proposals. If the venture capital firm does decide to invest, it goes through a standard procedure of deciding how much to invest, and the form of this investment including deciding on the structure of the investment and whether or not the venture capital firm would provide management supervision.

The essential core of successful venture capital investing is:

1. Discover which potential investments have a flat(ish) demand curve.
2. Whether the firm will operate under increasing returns to scale.

That's all.

Many hundreds of books have been written about successful venture capital investing. They go on and on about discerning risk, and ascertaining how much capital you require, discerning the capabilities and characters of your potential partners, how to motivate your employees. Yes, they can be important. But only if the enterprise is marginal. If the startup enterprise is highly profitable, a lot can and does be forgiven, at least for a while.

If the enterprise fits the first two criteria *above* it will rapidly take off

and:
1. If the enterprise is immediately successful, there is NO risk involved. (Less than going to work as an employee – as one entrepreneur told me, if thing go wrong, you will be the last to be fired.)
2. You won't require much capital, as Robert Kiyosaki says, (Kiyosaki (1992)), or in many circumstances, none at all. Forget the employee mindset "I need money". You will find that banks and money lenders will throw money at you from an early stage. You will after you have got going, like Steve Jobs, find it difficult to refuse investment offers.

3. The characters and capabilities of your partners. That is actually a killer. Very few people (less than 20%), from my experience, are naturally hardworking and honest. What keeps the rest on track is the necessity to earn a pay packet. Don't believe verbal promises. "A verbal promise is not worth the paper it written on".

   Instead of going down the psychology route, I have found the best method is to put everyone on employee mode. Put their promised goals on paper, together with penalties. Give them a copy. (They will laugh "ha,ha,ha" the first couple of times, then there will be clear resentment), but you say that "if you do not perform, our partnership will be terminated, as per our partnership agreement, blah, blah, blah". Tough, but it is better than crying later.

   However, it is best not to have partners. See the above paragraph about capital. Have a number of trusted paid employees. "A brains trust". But they work for a salary. They are used to it. It is also a very good idea to motivate staff by offering them shares in some form. You will be amazed how much this changes their attitude and performance.

4. Employee motivation. Hundreds of books have been written on this. But they are all United States centred. What if your factory is in China or Japan? Totally different. Even moving the production to Mexico leads to personnel problems. My advice is to find a local competent and experienced manager, and have local people in ALL management and supervisory roles. Indeed, if you have plants located in different parts of the United States, it is best to have all managers born and bred in that locality.

So, what does a flat demand curve look like? This is shown in Figure 26.

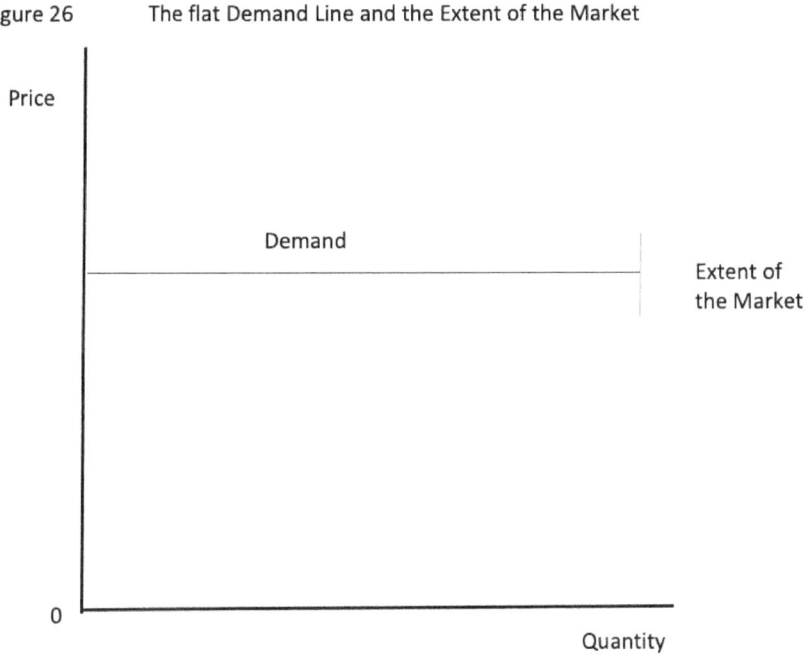

Figure 26   The flat Demand Line and the Extent of the Market

If you take price on one axis and quantity on the other, while in most cases the quantity sold will only increase when the price of the good decreases, with a flat demand curve the price for the good does not decline as the quantity sold increases, at least up to a certain point. In economic terms, this demand curve is called "perfectly elastic".

Is such a curve possible in practice? Of course. Bill Gates of Microsoft had such a flat demand curve. He had an almost infinite demand for his software at a given price throughout the world. All software products generally exhibit this characteristic. That is why software sellers often get rich very quickly.

It has been a rule of the thumb that for a venture capitalist investing in software, it was usually a lay down misere. However, the problem in recent times is that there is absolutely no demand for certain types of software – at any price. So, you have to test the market. But the risks are small. If the software does not initially sell, the loss is generally small.

All manufactured goods do not have a flat demand curve. Adam Smith got on top of this issue right away. The success of your enterprise depends on not only on "division of labour" but the "extent of the market". You can export. If you have a free trade area, exporting in containers is relatively cheap. That is why Chinese manufacturing has succeeded so well. Not because of cheap labour.

There are two diagrams a potential venture capitalist needs to keep in mind. There are two. Just two. It is pretty simple. The first, and most important, is the slope of the potential demand curve. Is it flat? The second is, the appearance of the returns to scale curve. At first, as you can see in Figure 27, you get increasing returns to scale, as you employ more people and you get increasing division of labour. The tasks are divided into small and smaller portions for each employee, and thus increase productivity. How long can this continue? This is a management problem. Sooner or later management gets slack and complaisant, and returns to scale stops and decreasing returns to scale starts. There is no intermediation of constant returns to scale.

This is not just a theoretical problem. After Steve Job's death, Apple, for example, back in 2013, went on an employment spending spree. The number of employees shot up. As a consequence, entered decreasing returns to scale. (See Table 1 above). As a consequence, Apple struggled for the next few years, and has never really recovered.

What are the two essential requirements for a startup?

Figure 27   The Two Diagrams that have to be kept in mind when investing in New Enterprises

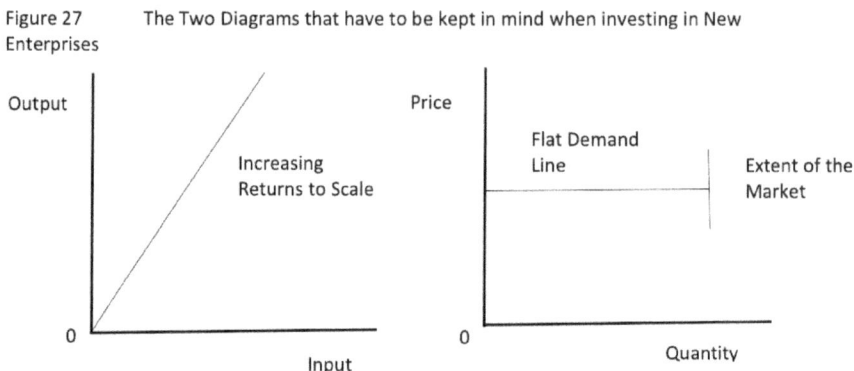

The above two diagrams are what the venture capitalist, or potential venture capitalists, should always keep in mind. All other issues, costs, debt (You really shouldn't have much), management, personnel issues, are really side issues compared to the above – demand for your product, and are you continuing to operate in increasing returns.

You must make absolutely sure that you can operate in and remain in increasing returns to scale. If you re-engineer the formulae in Chapter Fourteen. You can make sure of that. But you must retain complete control over all your internal production activities. Outsourcing it to some firm such as Foxconn is a recipe for disaster. It is as if you have a whole production division over which you do not control the inputs. What is worse, you do not gain the benefits of increasing returns to scale. Your contractor will offer you a fixed price contract. Whatever the consultants say, this behaviour is not in the least bit clever. They are your inputs. You must control them.

Yes, there is a limit to your market. It will become evident when you can only sell your product at lower prices. That is a worry. You need a new product.

Another piece of useful advice. The 80/20 rule. After your firm has grown past the eponymous 150 employee mark, you will find that 20 per cent of your products bring in 80 per cent of your profits, and indeed, 20 per cent of your employees, (usually the ones at the bottom), produce 80 percent of your profits. Your major job, as the guy at the top of a firm which may be running out of puff, is to identify both the best products and the best employees, and then go away, and decide what to do about it.

So, in summary, success in venture capitalism is almost solely due to two factors
- Whether the potential demand curve for your product has a flat or near flat demand curve
- Whether you can maintain production or output in the firm under increasing returns to scale.

Simple. But how many venture capital projects fail because they have not met one or more of these criteria? Certainly, all the failures. Bad management, high costs, or changing marketing conditions are just excuses.

CHAPTER TWENTY

THE VENTURE CAPITAL PROCESS

This chapter goes into more detail of the venture capital process. It has now become pretty standardised, as it has become an industry. Venture proposals in one end, startups out the other. And it is a highly profitable industry.

At this point any stories of the history and the current functioning of the venture capital market goes into jargon. The jargon and methodology have become standardised, but to a non-venture capitalist these terms are still a mystery. So, I have decided to start with the framework of venture capitalism, and a description how it works.

Table 3   The Venture Capital Process

The idea	It all starts here. The entrepreneur has an idea. Then the entrepreneur approaches an angel investor with his/her idea for financing. The entrepreneurs need not supply any financing for the enterprise.
Angel investing	A small amount of money. Nowadays this amount has increased in value up to $100,000. The angel investor help set up the company, and provides some element of advice and help.
Series A	After the enterprise has begun production and sales, this Series is the first set of investments from initial investors. The shares of the enterprise have increased in value, and the Series A investors pay an increased price per share.
Series B	The worth of the company has greatly expanded, and the Series B investors pay a much higher price per share. Total investment could be around $100 million.
IPO	Public float. The public is invited to invest in an issue of

shares in the company that will be traded on the stock exchange. From now on the company will be valued at this quoted share price.

The above is the basic investment structure that has evolved in the Venture Capital headquarters in Silicon Valley. There could be more Series of investment, Series C and so on, but this is unusual. There is a strong desire from investors to have an IPO (Initial Public Offer) quickly, so that they can cash out. Though many wait longer in the hope of obtaining an increased share price.

So, what is the description of the process?

"In the beginning was the idea, and the idea was with the entrepreneur".

The first step is that an entrepreneur has a potentially profitable idea. At this stage the idea may be just in his head, and not even on paper. There is not necessarily even a company, or even a business plan. (What's that?).

The next stage is that the entrepreneur wants to start production and sales, and for that he needs capital. He has to approach other potential investors. These initial investors are called Angel Investors.

Until very recently, Angel investors were few and fearful. But the market has evolved and massively changed. The supply of Angel investors has greatly increased, largely because of the initial influence of Paul Graham and his Angel investing firm Y-Combinator. (More of this later). Now that investors have seen how potentially profitable Angel investing can be, there are a large number of copyists. As a result, nowadays, your entrepreneur in most locations has little difficulty raising initial investments for a high proportion of proposals. This development has been highly beneficial for society and the economy as a whole.

While the initial investments of Angel investments are usually relatively small (though this amount has grown to be up to $100,000), the potential relative gains are high as the enterprise moves into Series A investment or Series B investment.

However, it must be stressed that a high proportion of Angel investments do not succeed at this point. Y-Combinator has published a useful list of reasons for enterprise failure. These are:

Table 4   Reasons for enterprise failure

1. There is no market need for the idea   42%
2. The enterprise runs out of cash   29%
3. The enterprise does not have the right team   23%
4. The enterprise gets outcompeted   19%
5. Pricing/cost issues   18%
6. Poor quality product   17%
7. The enterprise lacks a business model/plan   17%
8. Poor marketing   14%
9. The entrepreneurs ignore customer
    suggestions   14%
10. The product mis-timed/too early   13%
11. The management lose focus/get tired   13%
12. Pivot gone bad   10%
13. The entrepreneurs lack/lose passion   9%
14. Bad Location   9%

15. There is disharmony among team/investors 8%
16. No Financing due to lack of Investor Interest   8%
17. Legal Challenges   8%
18. The entrepreneurs don't use Network/Advisors   8%
19. Management burn out   8%
20. Failure to Pivot   7%

There can be two or more simultaneous reasons for failure.

Except for the first two reasons, no market and running out of cash, most of the reasons for failure are personal, not financial as was previously commonly supposed. Character problems and bad judgement. And even running out of cash is really caused by bad management and bad judgement.

As Peter Thiel, the VC investor, (discussed later) decided, it is not worth his time, effort and resources to sort out the personal issues of the enterprise founders. He discovered that the best policy for his VC firm was to fund a large number of startups, and let the failures die without putting in much effort to keep them alive.

A question many people ask is "What proportion of the initial startup's shares does the Angel investor get"? The answer is that this proportion has massively fallen from around 80% or more in the 1950's to about 6% with Y-Combinator. The trade-off is that while the VC of old would hunt around for highly paid CEO's to the manage the firm, and put up with the original company founders not washing, having board meetings in hot tubs and coming to meetings in pyjamas, nowadays this behaviour is not tolerated. These same founders are left to sink or swim. The VC calculation is that even if 90 out of 100 startups fail because of the behavioural failures of the company founders, they will still make a big profit.

The next step is Series A. Those firms that survive to this stage are hawked around among the Angel investor's list of wealthy individuals and interested organisations, and are asked if they are willing to invest in shares in this company. These individuals and organisations need to be legally capable to invest in these high-risk investments. This is a legal issue that varies from country to country, and I won't go into it. These investments are high risk because even at this stage the company could fail. However, these shares would even at this stage be worth a lot more than the Angel investor paid for them.

A related issue is whether these shares are a new issue, or taken from the existing stock of shares held by the Angel investor and the founders. From the economic point of view it makes no difference, but it is amazing how much the original shareholders and lawyers are hung up about this issue.

The firm continues to do well, and there is usually a second round of Share issues – Series B. Again, at a higher price. The buyers of these shares need not be the same sort of buyers as those for the Series A. But it is the same process. These early issues are high risk, but they can be very profitable.

This process can continue for Series C, Series D, and so on, but by this time the original shareholders would be getting toey and demanding an IPO.

The IPO, the Initial Public Offer, is something different. The shares are offered to the general public in a float, to be usually list on a Stock Exchange. An issue of new shares is usually made, and they are offered to the general public at either a fixed price, or more unusually, at some form of auction. The treatment varies though there is a general standard. The price of these shares exceeds the share prices paid by the original investors. It is often made certain that the founders and original investors have free bonus share allocated to them. There are also "vested" shares and share options for the founders and many employees. There is not set formula. Except that the outcome is usually highly profitable for the company founders and original investors.

Recently there has been an interesting development in the VC industry. The VCs are turning into large investment banks. The most successful Venture Capitalist companies, such as Peter Theil's Founders Funds or Paul Graham's Y-Combinator are now worth many billions of Dollars. The Wall Street Journal said on December 29 2022 that the venture capital industry had a stockpile of $539 billion cash. Due to their success, venture capital companies are rapidly transforming into large and very powerful investment banks. While normal investment banks make a good living trading in the financial markets, the venture capital participants are using investments in entrepreneurial companies to make money at a more rapid rate. Nevertheless, they will have to find a profitable short-term use for all this cash. As such they will begin to compete with the normal investment banks. VC companies have access to vast quantities of newly created wealth, while the best the normal investment banks can do is borrow funds or rely of many years of accumulated capital. If the venture capital companies are competently managed, they are likely to outcompete the previous model of investment banks. They already exceed their value.

CHAPTER TWENTY-ONE

THE HISTORY OF VENTURE CAPITAL

It is necessary to know how the Venture Capital industry evolved to understand how it operates. And evolved it did. The industry itself could have taken-off in several directions, and may have had many different types of investors. But evolution constrained it to one location at the start and one structure. And no, it was not a corporation. But once it opted on this successful format, the system was highly successful.

The Venture Capital industry did not start in Silicon Valley, nor did it start with the present structure. It started far away in Boston, in 1944, and its father was George Doriot, who established American Research and Development (ARD), a publicly listed venture vehicle. Doriot was a Harvard Business School professor. For each new enterprise, ARD would provide a $70,000 equity investment and a $30,000 loan in return for 70% of the company. ARD made a few successful investments such as Amgen and Digital Equipment Corporation, and the company multiplied the value of its original investment by 30 times. Nevertheless, ARD was a public company, and at the time this type of investment was not highly regarded by the investing public. As a result, its quoted share value was less than its accumulated liquidation value, so as a result, in 1972, ARD was liquidated. So, this type of VC company died.

On the West Coast, back in 1957, a revolt was brewing. The founder of Shockley Semiconductor Laboratory, William Shockley, was a despot. To cut the story short, after much misgiving, eight senior researchers left to start a new company,

Fairchild Semiconductor. The midwife was Arthur Rock, of what became the first genuine venture capital company, Heydon Stone. For this purpose, it raised money from Shane Fairchild, of Fairchild Cameras and Instruments. The "traitorous eight" were each asked to raise $500 for 500 $1 shares, and Fairchild raised $1.4 million, and obtained options to pay $3 million for the traitorous eight's shares. Three years later Fairchild exercised that option, paying each of the eight $600,000.

Arthur Rock's firm transformed into Davis and Rock, a limited partnership for taxation reasons, that also had a limited life. These partners included 6 of the 8 traitorous Fairchild engineers. Without going into too many details, they founded Intel, Data Systems and Teledyne among many other successful firms. Arthur Rock did very well, and was known to have a butler at his house above Palo Alto! Davis and Rock moved the VC industry to Sandhills Road in Silicon Valley. Another innovation was that Rock insisted that all initial employees be given shares or options in the startup. Later on, VC's started vesting these shares – that is delaying the allocation of tranches of these shares. However, this led to problems. A third innovation that Rock introduced was to impose an outside CEO on the startup. While this may appear necessary, it was an extra expense, and long VC experience showed that the imposition of outside CEO's on the founders had varied success.

The firm Davis and Rock was terminated in 1968. Both Davis and Rock retired, though Rock continued to have considerable influence in the VC industry.

The first permanent partnership was Kleiner Perkins, founded by Tom Perkins and Eugene Kleiner in 1972. Perkins was the general manager of Hewlett Packard's computer division while Kleiner was one of the traitorous eight previously discussed.

Perkins tracked down Kleiner and persuaded him to partner him in a VC enterprise. They raised $8.4 million and after a few unsuccessful startups, they started Tandem Computers, a systems software company, and then Genentech, a gene technology firm to produce artificial insulin. Both these companies were highly successful. With Genentech a new VC technique evolved. This was to deal with what Perkins called "dealing with white hot risks" at a staged rate. The biggest technological and scientific risks were identified stage by stage, and instead of giving the startup a large sum at the start, limited funding was also provided stage by stage. In the case of Genentech, most of the research was outsourced by contract, as the firm itself owned limited facilities.

By this time a number of copycat Venture Capitalists had started. The most outstanding at this date was Sequoia Capital, founded by Don Valentine in 1974. He started his career at Fairchild Semiconductor, moved to the startup National Semiconductor, was recruited by an investment fund Capital Research and Management, and then in 1974 decided to start his own VC, Sequoia Capital. He raised $5 million from various sources, including Rockefeller University, then cast around for a suitable startup. He found Atari, manufacturer of the primitive computer game Pong. The eccentric owners had discouraged other potential VC investors, but Valentine persevered. Sequoia invented the first Series A investment, and then sold Atari to Warner Brothers for a good profit. The next of Sequoia's successes was Cisco, another firm with strange entrepreneurs that they fostered. The founders of Cisco, Leonard Bosack and Sandy Lerner, were highly eccentric. Bosack was autistic while Lerner had a habit of calling employees "brain dead". Nevertheless, Cisco's product, a software system that coordinated different software and made them talk to each other, was in massive demand. In the end, there was another employee revolt. Valentine was told by all the Cisco engineers, "Either Lerner goes, or we go". Lerner went. Unfortunately, as she had not lasted her full contracted employment term, she lost one third of her vested shares.

By this time, the early 90's, the VC structure was pretty well established. Angel investing, Series A, Series B, IPO. There were a few highly profitable investments, a larger number of moderately successful investments, and a tail of unprofitable ventures. The success record followed a "power law" as below.

Figure 28   The Power Curve of Venture Capital Revenues

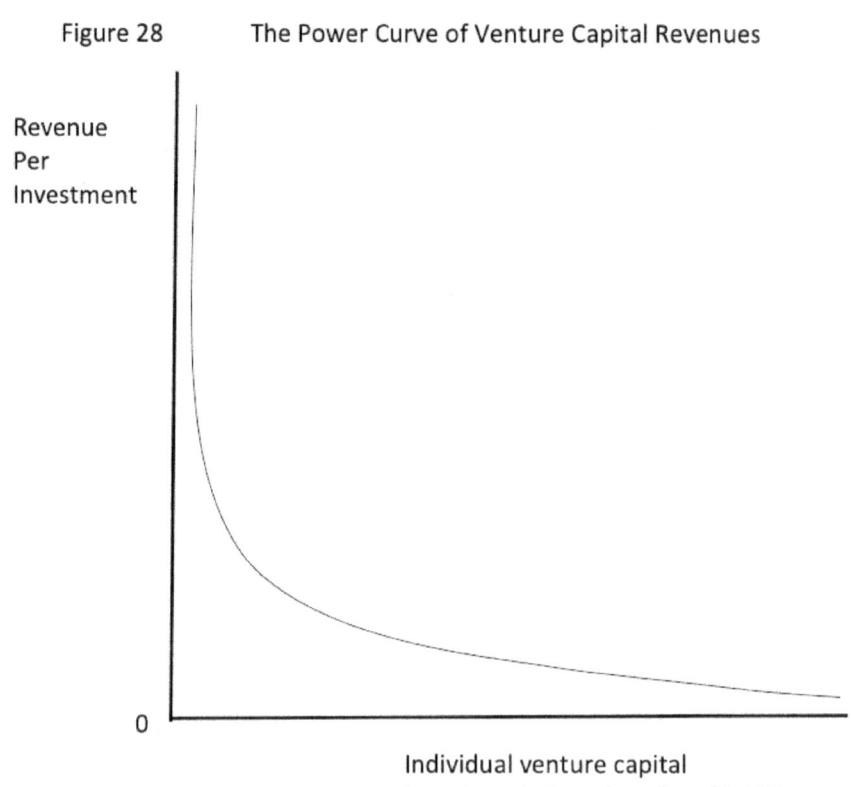

Revenue
Per
Investment

0

Individual venture capital
investments in order of profitability

In the VC business, the bonanzas (in VC parlance "the unicorns") are few. There are a far greater number of moderate successes, and a very large number of unprofitable failures.

As an aside (another aside!), many venture investors go by the 80/20 rule, as advocated by Richard Koch who wrote a book on this subject. He claimed his financial fortune grew using this rule. Only 20% of venture investments are worthwhile. A useful rule of the thumb, maybe, but the power law is a lot more informative. But you do need precise data if you are involved in large scale investment. Y-Combinator has it, but they are not giving it out.

The VC company has to set the gains against the losses. However, by carefully controlling the losses, even quickly closing down enterprises that were failing, the average venture capital company at the time made an average gain of 20% per annum. And there was a chance of making a major gain. All that was required was to follow the established system. The VC industry was mature and highly profitable.

But the VC industry changed again. It evolved into a system of large-scale support for start-up entrepreneurs. It was not realised at the time, but entrepreneurs themselves were a vast source of wealth, unicorns or not. The source of wealth was entrepreneurialism. The first to supply this large-scale support (by near accident) was Peter Thiel in the late 1990's. By 2022 he was reputed to be the richest man in the United States. Another, Paul Graham, set up what was intended to be a near charity to support startups, Y-Combinator, in 2005, and by 2022 Y-Combinator was worth $14 billion. This pair had hit on the philosopher's stone! Supporting large numbers of entrepreneurs with few restrictions was a vast source of wealth.

The more entrepreneurs, the more money they made. The old days of careful selection and supervision were gone.

Peter Thiel had two degrees from Stanford, drifted in and out of derivatives trading in New York, drifted back to the West Coast, started a small hedge fund, and contributed to the libertarian Stanford Review. After giving a lecture on currency trading at Stanford, he met Steve Levchin who pitched him the idea of starting a cryptography company. They pivoted to starting an encrypted payments company, with Elon Musk. They came into competition with a firm supported by Sequoia. After some antagonism, they were persuaded by Sequoia to merge 50:50, with the name PayPal. A couple of years later PayPal went public. Shortly after that Elon Musk was fired as Chairman. He walked away with $150 million.

In 2005, Thiel launched Founders Fund. This fund had a new philosophy. Instead of the VC bringing in an outside CEO, entrepreneurs would control their own companies. But Thiel went further. And I am quoting Sabastian Mallaby from his book the "Power Law". He cited the Pareto 80/20 rule. He observed that radically unequal outcomes were common in the natural and social world. It was therefore not just a curiosity that a single venture capital bet could dominate the entire portfolio. It was a natural law. He argued that venture capitalists should stop monitoring founders. The power law dictated that the companies would have to be exceptional outliers. Thiel felt that the founders of these outstanding startups were necessarily so gifted that a bit of VC coaching would barely change their performance. He found that the strongest performers were the companies that he had the least amount of engagement with. The art of venture capital was to find rough diamonds, not to spend time polishing them.

Thiel went further. He said that to the extent that VC coaching did make a difference, it might well be negative. When venture capitalists imposed their methods on founders, they were implicitly betting that tried-and-tested formulas trumped outside the box experiments. If the power law said that only a handful of truly original contrarian startups were destined to succeed, it made no sense to suppress idiosyncrasies. To the contrary, venture capitalists should embrace contrarian and singular founders, the wackier the better.

Entrepreneurs who weren't oddballs would create businesses that were simply too normal. They would come up with a sensible plan that would have occurred to others. Consequently, they would find themselves in a niche that was too crowded and competitive to allow for big profits. Because only handful of startups would grow exponentially, there was no point in getting excited about opportunities that seemed merely solid.

Mentoring had a cost, from the diversion of the VC's time from more profitable ventures, to the actual extra economic cost of this mentoring. Also, Peter Thiel has been quoted as saying "Get rid of non-performing CEO's and employees early. Leopards do not change their spots."

Founders Fund thus was a low-cost VC, that spent minimally on mentoring its proteges. They either sank or swim. On the other hand, Founders Fund had a record of funding a large number and a wide variety of investment proposals, the wilder the better, such as Uber. A significant proportion proved to be highly successful, making Peter Thiel very rich indeed.

As an aside, Thiel invested with Elon Musk on Tesla and SpaceX. To date these have been very profitable investments.

The next development in the Venture Capital industry was due to Paul Graham. While Peter Thiel was still rooted in the venture capital industry, although he spread his investments far and wide, Paul Graham made the jump into Angel Investing.

In 1995, Graham together with a fellow Harvard graduate student, started a software company called Viaweb, selling it in 1998 to Yahoo for $45 million of stock. He then turned his hand to writing, denigrating venture capitalists. "Spend as little as you can, because every dollar of investors money you will get it taken out of your ass". "What I discovered was that business was no great mystery. Build something that users love, and spend less than you make. How hard is that?". He was also strongly against large investments in startups. He said this caused dithering and distraction, and nervous VC's installed humourless MBAs to oversee quirky coders, much as the Bolsheviks foisted political commissars on Red Army units. Sweeping these criticisms together, Graham propounded what he called "a unified theory of VC suckage." "The VC is a classic villain: alternatively cowardly, greedy, sneaky, and overbearing." "When startups need less money, investors have less power….The VCs will have to be dragged kicking and screaming down this road, but like many things people have to be dragged. Kicking and screaming toward, it may be really good for them."

Graham, except for his polemics against venture capitalists, semi-retired. In March 2005 he gave a lecture to the Harvard computer society titled "How to Start a Startup". After giving his usual polemics, he was approached by two students, Alexis Ohanian and Steve Huffman who had travelled from the University of Virginia to see him. They had a proposal to write a program that allowed people to order food by text message, and asked to have coffee with him. Which he did.

Four days later, Graham and his girlfriend, Jessica Livingston, were walking across Harvard Square, and he thought about his meeting with the two students. Why not help young founders by giving back? Set up an organisation to do a little bit of Angel Investing?

Over the next couple of days, the pair came up with a novel plan for seed investing. It would plug the gap that Graham saw in mainstream venture capital. There would be minimal startup investment. It would be a summer school for aspiring entrepreneurs. They would all get together. Each participant would get $6000 to sustain them for three months of programming. They would also receive practical and emotional help; how to incorporate a company, open company bank accounts, and advise about patents. They would obtain feedback from the other participants, and there would be dinner once a week. The name of this organisation would be "Y-Combinator", which is a mathematical term for a circular method.

In the course of time, Y-Combinator grew and became a full-time organization for angel investing. It expanded to Palo Alto, and it is now located in virtually every major city in the world. Aside from concentrating on angel investing, another innovation was its total share of the startup's final share capital would be only 6 per cent. However, like the Founders Fund, intervention in the management of these startups would be strictly hands off. Aside from requested advice, it would be strictly sink or swim. Survival of the fittest. The struggling and unprofitable firms soon expired. The profitable went on to

Series A, Series B and the IPO. Y-Combinator also profited from this process.

Between 2005 and 2022 Y-Combinator proved to be highly profitable, making a total profit of $14 billion. It was responsible, for instance, for setting up Airbnb. The success of Y-Combinator surprised Paul Graham, who is quoted as saying that this profit was "not intended". He had set up Y-Combinator for the benefit of intending entrepreneurs, not his own profit.

Since then, a number of copyists, such as Techstars, Seedcamp, Pioneer, and Entrepreneurs First, have set up. The latter company has sprouted offices in London, Berlin, Paris, Singapore, Hong Kong and Bangalore.

The question arises, why was Y-Combinator so successful? The answer goes back to Figure 24, The Power Curve of VC Profits. The essential feature of this curve is that while just a few of these new enterprises are wildly successful, there is a much greater number who lost money. Y-Combinator's success is due to the large number of potential entrepreneurs it attracts and fosters. Also, as described in the next Chapter, successful entrepreneurs create wealth. Entrepreneurialism is the source of wealth. VC entrepreneurs tap into this vast and perpetual source of wealth creation.

In Y-Combinator the initial enterprises get limited initial funding in the Thiel style, and unlike the original style of Sequoia Capital minimal resources are spent on management. If the original entrepreneurs prove incapable of managing their new enterprise from the start, and there is no rapid growth, most of the enterprises are allowed to fail. There is no patience nowadays for hot bath board meetings, pyjama clad get togethers, or eccentric founders; the curating of badly run startups has ceased.

To date, the Venture Capital industry has evolved a successful and viable methodology. From the original recruitment of a few isolated genius' at a restricted location, the Venture Capital industry has transformed into a form of mass production of VC enterprises. Profits are now just a matter of numbers. Many are called. Few succeed, but those few succeed wildly. The rest fall by the wayside – bad or incomplete ideas, bad management, bad luck.

Nevertheless, this form of investment has been found to be wildly successful for many VC entrepreneurs.

To summarise, the basic methodology of the venture capital firm is as follows:

Table 5   The basic methodology of the venture capital firm

1. The purpose of Venture Capital is to assist the entrepreneur to start a business to utilise his idea, and make money for both of them, by providing startup capital, advice and maybe management.
2. The Venture Capitalist starts its business by setting up a VC organisation.
3. The Venture Capitalist advertises for/attracts entrepreneurs.
4. The VC sifts through applications. While early VCs were highly selective, the policy of Y-Combinator and the like is to be less selective, and to prefer original investment ideas.

5. Early VCs provided management guidance. The latest idea of Peter Thiel and Paul Graham is to provide minimal to no management guidance.
6. The aim is to get big fast, in an area where there is no competition. For that reason, the idea has to be original.
7. From the shape of the power curve, it can be seen that the major profits are made from the few highly profitable startups. The vast bulk of firms in the tail prove to be unprofitable.

Yes, ideas are cheap. Most are not original. But as Paul Graham says, among them are rough diamonds. The role of the venture capitalist is to expose this rough diamond, and to fashion it to create new wealth, not only for the venture capitalist and the entrepreneur, but for society as a whole.

CHAPTER TWENTY-TWO

HOW DO ENTREPRENEURS CREATE WEALTH?

This question is the basic question. Do entrepreneurs create wealth that did not previously exist? How is this done?

To explain how wealth is created, we need to go back to the question of the role of increasing returns to scale. In economics, everything goes in a full circle, and everything is interconnected.

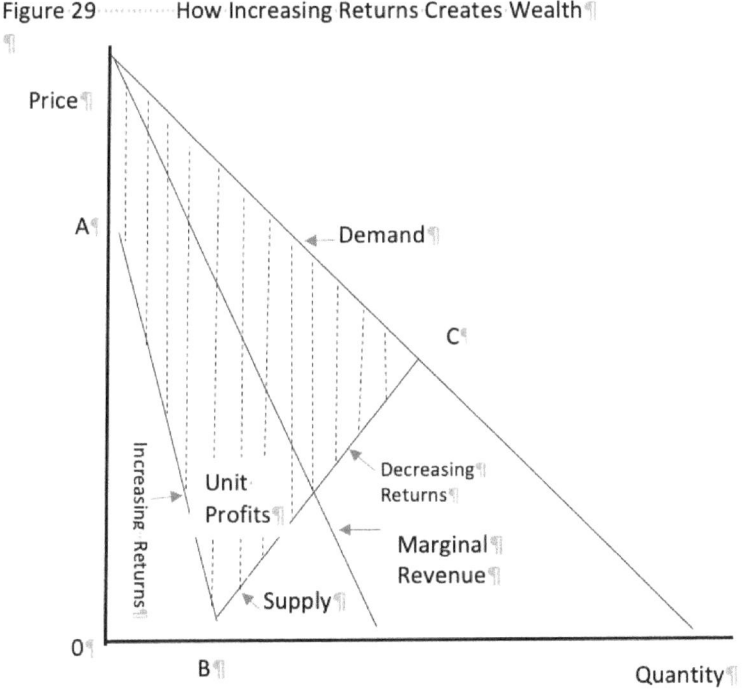

Figure 29 ·········· How Increasing Returns Creates Wealth

As the above diagram shows, the unit profit of a product is the length of the line from the Supply line or MC line, FDE, the Demand line, AB. From F to D, as the length of this line lengthens, the number of unit profits increase. Total profit at each point is the unit profit at that point times the quantity sold. This total profit does not reach a maximum until the MC lie crosses the MR line. Although unit profits are then declining the quantity sold is increasing. Unit and total profits decline to zero when the MC line touches the Demand line.

However, as long as the firm stays on increasing returns, its unit profits increases – unless the Demand line is very steep, steeper than the marginal cost line. But normally, most Demand is elastic and the supply line under increasing returns to scale stays well under the Demand line. That is, the supply price stays well under the sale price.

This raises the question, is aggregate wealth increased by entrepreneurial activity? Also, is wealth destroyed elsewhere in the economy?

In answer to the first question, If the activity of an individual entrepreneur creates wealth, then if there are numerous entrepreneurs active, then wealth is created by the sum total of all their activities. The more active entrepreneurs, the more wealth is created, if each entrepreneur creates a finite positive amount of wealth. Roughly, wealth is created in direct proportion of the number of active entrepreneurs.

The profit of an individual entrepreneurial firm is proportional to the distance of the marginal revenue line from the supply line. Increased competition has the effect of decreasing prices, and thus reducing profits, as the demand and the marginal revenue lines are pushed towards the supply line. Also, the supply curve could be moved upwards, as increased competition for inputs could increase the price of inputs. All round, increased competition reduces profits.

However, the belief that there is a fixed quantity of profits that all the firms divide is total nonsense. Increased competition, while decreasing sales prices, increases sales. Depending on the likely elasticity of demand, reduced prices by increasing sales could, and from experience likely, to increase aggregate profits.

In summary, one of the most certain methods of creating wealth is to start a new firm where the selling price of your product is greater than the price at which the product is produced. This is the most certain, the most universal method of wealth creation.

Yes, there are other ways to gain wealth. Speculation, thievery, conquest, and other non-productive activities such as litigation. Speculation has only 50% chance of success. It is a zero-sum game at the best. A well-run society reduces profits of thievery and other non-productive activities to a supportable maximum. (And that includes thievery by the government and the legal system!) As for conquest......In the past, when wealth was gold there was a chance. Nowadays, wars destroy the productive capacity of the conquered, and there is no profit in wars of conquest. Even wars to gain so-called "wealth" such as oil supplies have proved un-profitable.

The advantage from starting a firm that exhibits increasing returns to scale is that, as Paul Romer pointed out, growth is automatically built in. Only when the firm hits decreasing returns to scale that the firm ceases to expand. Even with inefficiencies, the firm continues to grow under increasing returns to scale. The wealth of the entrepreneur continues to grow. It is well known that only when the firm hits the traces and stops expanding (hits the decreasing returns to scale phase) that the management is forced to prune a bloated work force.

As Adam Smith wrote, 250 years ago, in the "Wealth of Nations", Division of Labour (increasing returns to scale), and the extent of the market, is the source of all wealth.

So, to conclude, how do you become wealthy?

Become an entrepreneur.

That sounds trite, and you ask if there is a bit more to that?

Being an entrepreneur contains a number of things.

1. You must be creative. You have to think of at least one original money-making idea.
2. You must be proactive. You must flesh this idea out into a practical scheme, and yes, put this plan on paper. If the idea is for a physical product, build a prototype.
3. You must be hardworking. Before the scheme gets going, and much more afterwards, you must put in a lot of hard work. Commitment.

Did I say, you must put in capital? The archetypical 'capitalist'. No, not any more.

There is a <u>market</u> for good original ideas AND, combined with, a person with character, who is willing to work hard and put the idea into effect. Even at this stage, the combined idea and a suitable person, is worth money, a lot of money, to Venture Capitalists. No, you don't need to put up any money yourself.

From that stage forward, as long as you continue to produce the product under increasing returns to scale, and sell the product to your maximum ability, your firm will continue to expand rapidly. When will it stop expanding? For two reasons. You either hit decreasing returns to scale, which is really bad management, or you hit the extent of the market.

A surprisingly high number of entrepreneurs get very rich, very fast. But even if you just become moderately well off; with hard work, good management and a modicum of good luck, you will become far wealthier than remaining an employee.

CHAPTER TWENTY-THREE

THE IDEA

Back in Chapter Nineteen, in the description of the Venture Capital process, Table 3 laid out a diagram of the Venture Capital process from the start to finish. Right at the beginning was "The Idea". The Idea is the inception of the Enterprise. This is the foundation of all growth, our standard of living higher than the level of starvation, and indeed all human development. Three hundred years ago most of humanity lived just above starvation level. If you don't believe me, read Malthus (1820).

Ideas matter. Paul Romer said "What is the bigger obstacle to growth? A shortage of ideas or a shortage of things? It is a shortage of ideas."

The Idea, or more precisely ideas that are worth money, are the basis of civilisation. I cannot overemphasise this point. Human culture? As the saying goes, every poet has eaten once that day. It is the economy that matters most. And the function of the economy is ultimately based on ideas that are worth money.

I know earlier I said "Ideas are cheap". Yes, the production of ideas is cheap. It just takes a little effort, brain activity, and time. That is the only cost. But good ideas, once produced, are valuable. As Peter Thiel said, they have the value of rough diamonds. The value creation process starts at the point of the creation of ideas.

Some ideas come naturally. The spring into mind during a walk, as James Watt's idea did for the design of a steam engine. The unconscious mind is a major source of ideas. It has been found that if you think long and hard about a subject, the solution or idea pops into your head when you are sleeping, (like it did for August Kekulé with his Benzene rings), or during your awake moments in bed, (have paper and pencil beside your bed to record the idea), in the shower, or during walks. According to mythology, many ideas come in relaxed moments after a lot of thought.

But like all things, including the process of venture capital, a production process can be devised. Ideas can be produced on call. How does one do this? Isaac Newton described his method to create scientific ideas such as gravity. He thought long and hard on a subject (often sitting on the side of the bed all night), and the idea pops into his mind. It really does work.

But if you have no wish to do this, a methodology has been described in a book, written by Andy Boynton, Bill Fischer and William Bole called *The Idea Hunter*, that applies method to the process of finding ideas. I shall describe it.

They hang their methodology on a skeleton or mnemonic, using the word IDEA.

I is for being Interested across a wide as possible area as possible, and draw connections. Be curious. Ideas don't spring to your attention on their own. You need to draw together many different related ides. Put them together to solve a necessary problem, and you have an idea.

Albert Einstein said "I have no special talents. I am only curious". He brought together his interest in trains with the question of why the speed of light was the same in all directions, to discover Relativity.

On this question of interests, you yourself have a set of core interests, that Boynton et. al. call your "gig". This shortens your search for ideas. You gig is not necessarily your job, but what is your passion or purpose in life. What do I want to be? What do I stand for? What do I stand for? Does my work matter? Do I want to make a difference?

Is your vocation a source of joy? Is this something that taps into your talents and gifts? Is this a role a genuine service to the people around you?

D is for Diverse. This follows from the previous section. You need wide interests. Ideas are everywhere. They are like radio waves. You are surrounded by radio waves. Tap into them.

One of the best sources of information comes from a diverse network of contacts – called 'strong ties' and 'weak ties'. Strong ties are family and close associates. Weak ties are occasional contacts. Weak ties are more useful, as they have more diverse interests than strong ties. It has been found that weak ties are one of the best sources of entrepreneurial ideas. Chatting to someone at a bar can be more useful than talking to your family and close friends.

E is for Exercised. Work at it. You need to constantly exercise your mind, keep noticing things, thinking about what you have observed, and drawing conclusion. Do things. Don't turn off! Louis Pasteur said "Chance favours the prepared mind". Observe. Keep looking. Soon your mind will put two and two together and come up with an original idea.

Also, and an additional tip. Write it down. Writing down your thoughts and observations and keeping them readily accessible is important. Ideas tend to arrive in bits and pieces and need to be put back together over time. Most people do not have photographic memories. It is an additional benefit that you go over these written notes, and try to put them together. Thomas Edison for example recorded thoughts in more than 2,500 notebooks. He didn't feel pressure to organise the notes immediately, but let his thought processes develop naturally over days, months, and years. He invented moving pictures by combining photos with thoughts on the spiral grooves of phonographic records.

Whatever is your form of note-taking, it is best to take notes when the observation is fresh in your mind.

Lastly, in this section on Exercised, *prototype* your idea as soon as possible. While a picture is worth a thousand words, a working model, a physical object (if such is possible), or a piece of working software, is worth many thousands of words. Imperfect though it may be, a prototype is a big step along the way.

All working inventions need to start with a prototype. Prototypes knock out unseen errors at an early stage. It does not need to look pretty. Just the idea is made to work. It also creates something that other persons can evaluate. A prototype makes the idea more understandable and allows people to offer feedback.

A is for Agile. A is the last letter in IDEA. Getting moving with the idea is more important than the idea itself. How many people get a good idea, but do nothing about it!

We come to the fundamental required characteristic of an entrepreneur, ACTION.

So, you get an idea, but it is too painful to take the next step?

Take action!

What is your motivation? Answer the first four question yes, and the last no.

1. Do I enjoy spending time and energy on the idea? <u>Lots</u> of time and <u>lots</u> of energy. Go out there and talk to your friends about the idea (at least).
2. Deep down, do I really want to be a member of the project? (ie It is a good idea, but it is not really my scene. I don't like getting my hands dirty, or giving people orders and making sure that they obey the orders).
3. Will I learn something in the effort? If you don't want to learn, go back to bed.
4. Do I want to be known as the person who brought the idea to life? Do you prefer anonymity? (Most do). Fame, even in a small area, may not be desirable. Some people may hate you, or may be just jealous.
5. Can I imagine a set of circumstances in which I would prefer not to be associated with this idea? Going back over the previous questions , is it a case of "I want the money, but not the job".

Assuming that you answered 1 to 4 and 5 no, what do I do next?

1. Write the idea down. Describe it in detail.
2. Prototype it if you can. A physical working model/working piece of software is a major advance.

3. Obtain some Intellectual Property Rights, such as a Patent, Copyright, Trade Mark, what have you. In most countries the initial patent process can be quite cheap. Even software can be protected. At this stake see a Patent Attorney for advice. Not expensive, and well worth it.

Why go to all this trouble right at the beginning? Because there are denizens in the undergrowth who will <u>steal</u> your ideas. While the idea may not be worth much to you, to others the idea can be valuable, very valuable. Remember Peter Thiel's rough diamonds. Once you have obtained Intellectual Property Right protection, you can be less paranoid. For most countries in the world, you are, to a degree, protected.

4. While you are doing all this, write a Business Plan. Business Plans are not described in this book. You can get this information in loads of other books. You just need a simple business plan. Keep the message simple. Focus on the possible benefits to the stakeholders.

As again, Peter Thiel says "...in these proposals I look first at the idea at the start, then I just glance at the business plan, and then turn to the applicant's C.V. at the end. The business plan is just to give an idea of the applicant's competence."

5. No, you don't need money, capital, management expertise etc. All these you can get from the Angel Investor/Venture Capital company.

Look around. Nowadays there are many different Angel Investors. (My favourite was Y Combinator, but as it has grown it has become more bureaucratic. Nowadays you have to do a three-month course in management at San Francisco, no less! You can do better).

If the idea is good and original, and well described, many Angel Investors can be interested. You will almost certainly get a generous deal.

From then on, your hand will be held. Maybe. Yes, you will have to work hard, but do what you are told. Act sanely and rationally. Remember the Venture Capitalist may be greedy, but he has your interests, as well his own, in sight.

After this, is this idea your last? Remember, while you are working for the firm, all the ideas you propose are owned by the firm. After you leave the firm, (hopefully after you have made your pile), your ideas are your own. The pot need not have run dry. Go through the process again.

CHAPTER TWENTY-FOUR

APPLYING THE ENTERPRISE QUOTIENT E

As seen in Chapter Thirteen, Paul Romer's final equation (5) can be adjusted using E, the Enterprise Quotient, to be

$$\frac{\dot{A}_t}{A_t} = \theta s_t \overline{H} E \qquad (5a)$$

Where A_t is the stock of ideas

$\dot{A}_t$ = $\dfrac{dA_t}{d_t}$ is the flow of ideas

A_t =   the amount of human capital devoted to research

H_{At} =   the amount pf human capital devoted to research

$\overline{H}$ =   units of human capital that can be used to produce either consumer goods or ideas (constant)

S_t = $\dfrac{H_{At}}{\overline{H}}$

the fraction of the stock of human capital that is devoted to research

E =   Enterprise Quotient

θ =   parameter $\theta > 0$

Now when you include E, θ is redundant.

So (5a) can be converted to (6).

$$\frac{\dot{A_t}}{A_t} = s_t \overline{H} E \tag{6a}$$

or

$$\frac{\dot{A_t}}{A_t} = H_{At} E \tag{7a}$$

as

$$S_t. = \frac{H_{At}}{\overline{H}}$$

Thus

$$E = \frac{\dot{A_t}}{A_t \, H_{At}} \tag{8a}$$

Thus, the value of the Enterprise Quotient is the flow of ideas divided by the product of the stock of ideas times the amount of human capital devoted to research. In other words, the enterprise quotient is directly dependent on the flow of ideas, and is reduced for a "rich" country having a large stock of ideas and a large amount of human capital devoted to research. However, this implies that the flow of ideas is independent of the stock of ideas and the amount of human capital. But it is likely that there is a strong feed-back from the denominator to the numerator. Not all that previous research may be useless. However, to the extent that the previous stock of subsidised stock of research is useless for the purpose of creating new ideas, then the Enterprise Quotient E is reduced.

Now, the question is, how can suitable proxies be found that equation (8) can be converted to a fraction that can be derived from existing data.

A proxy for $\dot{A_t}$ can be assumed to be the number of patent *applications* made in a particular country. This is different from the number of patents *approved* by each country's patent office. Firstly, the number of patent applications can be approximately the same as the degree of entrepreneurial spirit in the economy, while the number of patents approved depends on the rigorousness of the respective country's patent office. This can vary between countries.

Statistics show that the US Patent Office is the most rigorous, rejecting the highest proportion of patent applications, while other countries such as Australia reject a smaller proportion of patent applications. Thus, the number of patents accepted is likely to be a poor proxy of the amount of enterprise in the country.

In regard to the ratio $\dot{A}_t / A_t$, unfortunately no patent office around the world seems to publish figures for the current stock of active patents A_t. There is no figure for the relationship between the number of patent applications and the stock of active patents.

The best proxy for this ratio appears to be the proportion of patent applications to number of the country's population. The higher this proportion, the higher the likely value of $\dot{A}_t / A_t$. Let's call this proportion

$$B = \frac{\dot{A}_t}{\text{population.}} \qquad (9a)$$

B has to be related to the quantity H_{At}, the amount spent on research, or R&D expenditure. As the size of a country increases, generally more is spent on research. This has to be brought into a simple relationship, so different countries can be easily compared. The simplest way to do this is to divide H_{At} by the GDP of each country. Lets call this variable

$$C = \frac{H_{At}}{GDP.} \qquad (10a)$$

$$E = \frac{\dot{A}_t}{A_t \, H_{At}} \qquad (11a)$$

Modify (8a) to derive the common ratio of E for each country.

$$E = \frac{B}{C} \qquad (12a)$$

From statistical data, E can be calculated for different values for a number of different countries in the following table:

Table 6   Calculating the Enterprise Quotient for various countries

COUNTRY	R&D EXPENDITURE AS A % OF GDP	NUMBER OF PATENT APPLICATIONS	POPULATION	PATENT APPLICATIONS /POPULATION	E ENTERPRISE QUOTIENT	E x 10³
	C			B	B/C	
USA	3.38	595,780	339,123,510	0.01757682	0.0051976	5.20
CHINA	2.44	1,585,667	1,425,840,886	0.001112098	0.00045578	0.46
UK	2.4	58,410	67,736,806	0.00086230	0.0003592	0.36
CANADA	1.7	77,165	38,781,806	0.0009583	0.000563	0.56
AUSTRALIA	1.83	33,409	25,978,935	0.0014399	0.0007868	0.79
FRANCE	2.35	72,800	64,256,584	0.0011329	0.000482	0.48
GERMANY	3.1	173,220	83,294,637	0.0020796	0.000670	0.67
INDIA	0.7	61,573	1,432,338,288	0.0042987	0.0061410	6.1
MEXICO	0.3	1305	128,455,567	0.0001315	0.000338	0.33
JAPAN	3.26	727,348	123,454,567	0.0589167	0.0180724	18.07

The implication of this table is that if a country does not make a full use of its R&D, its enterprise quotient would be low. A high rate of R&D does not guarantee a high enterprise quotient. On the other hand, a country like India that has a limited amount of R&D but has a high proportion of patent applications has a high Enterprise quotient E.

E is the proxy for the entrepreneurial spirit of each country. Of course, it does not cover total entrepreneurial activity in areas not covered by R&D, such as starting up shops, trucking companies and so on. Maybe suitable proxies for these activities can be found from further research.

Nevertheless, these results are interesting. It is not surprising that Japan is shown to be the most enterprising economy, with an E of 18.07. What is surprising is that India has an E that comes second, with an E of 6.1. The USA has an E of 5.20, despite its vast expenditure on R&D. China is shown to have an E of 0.46, an average level of enterprise activity, despite its high level of R&D activity. The UK shows a relatively poor level of entrepreneurial activity with an E of 0.36, around the same level as Mexico with an E of 0.33.

As has been said, the measure of E does not reflect areas of enterprise not related to R&D, such as starting shops and similar traditional enterprises. More research needs to be done to find proxies for these activities.

SUMMARY

This book is divided into Part I and Part II. Part I describes the theoretical aspects and Part II describes the more practical aspects of wealth creation.

I shall recapitulate what was said in the book. We started with basic microeconomics. At the start of this story, we proceed to demolish the standard narrative of microeconomics – the straight-line standard supply-demand diagram. Such a diagram is not correct for either an individual firm or when aggregated to a market under perfect competition. For the individual firm, the price is set when the supply curve contacts the marginal revenue curve. Under perfect competition, the supply line, not the demand line, is horizontal, and the horizontal supply line meets a downward sloping demand line.

We moved on to discuss this concept of increasing returns to scale. We show that the supply curve mostly goes in a downward direction, with a short up-tick of decreasing returns to scale at the end. Decreasing returns then ceases when it touches the Marginal Revenue line, when the firm ceases to make a profit. The largest area of profit is when the firm operates under increasing returns to scale. That is the goal of profitable operations.

During this part of the story, I showed that constant returns to scale did not exist, as there is theoretically or in practice a flat line between the increasing returns and decreasing returns lines. From the point of view of the book, this is a side issue. But an important one. Due to the economic profession's obsession with this nonsensical concept, constant returns to scale, over two hundred years, that most important economic concept, increasing returns to scale, was totally neglected.

The book then describes Paul Romer's Nobel Prize winning increasing returns model. The so-called endogenous growth model. Romer divided the variables of his model into rival and non-rival goods. Rival goods were traditional goods that appear in economics, including capital, labour, human capital etc. Romer attributed knowledge to be a non-rival good. Regardless of how apiece of knowledge is used, the full amount could be used again and again without a reduction in quantity. From this insight Romer produced a production function that operates under increasing returns to scale.

Romer's model was adapted to include an Enterprise Quotient, E. E was taken to mean the measure of Enterprise, the entrepreneurial push or spirit in the economy. When added to Romer's model it increased the extent of the degree of increasing returns to scale, and thus reinforces the process of the creation of wealth.

Part II delves into the role of entrepreneurs, entrepreneurialism, Venture Capital, and the creation of wealth.

The first chapter of this section commences with a definition of Enterprise. That is Enterprise is the action to start a firm to produce and sell a good or service, and it is intended that this firm would operate under increasing returns to scale.

This chapter then goes on to relate Enterprise to Romer's model and increasing returns to scale, and through that the creation of wealth. Enterprise, Returns to Scale and the creation of wealth are ineluctably tied up. The value of wealth is drawn from the creation of wealth, and not from some physical stock value.

The book then goes on to discuss the definition of the Entrepreneur. "An Entrepreneur is a person who takes action to start a firm that will operate under increasing returns to scale to produce and sell goods and services". It is noted that an integral component of the above definition is increasing returns to scale. With increasing returns to scale, an entrepreneur's firm would not create wealth for himself and society. The chapter then goes on to describe the essential characteristics of an entrepreneur.

This chapter is followed by the history of the name "Entrepreneur". It starts with Cantillon (1725), who invented the name. And then goes through Adam Smith (1776), and describes the demise in the use of the name and concept for a further 100 years until Alfred Marshall (1890), Frank Knight (1921), Schumpeter (1934) until Baumol (1968). From the 1980's there was a relative (relative to the past) explosion in the use of the name from Casson (1982) to Parker (2018). None the less, the comparison with total economics publications remain small.

We move on to Venture Capital investing. The venture capital firm receives proposals from persons interested in undertaking entrepreneurial activities from outside the firm, assesses them, and decides whether or not to invest in these proposals. If the venture capital firm does decide to invest, it goes through a standard procedure of deciding how to invest, and the form of this investment includes deciding on the structure of the investment and whether the venture capital firm would provide management supervision. This chapter describes the investment criteria used.

The next chapter describes the venture capital process, including the description of the framework of venture capital investing from Angel investing through Series A and B, to the IPO. This chapter finishes with a list of the usual reasons for failure of venture capital investment.

The following chapter is the history of venture capital from the start in Silicon Valley, California, in the 1950's to Paul Graham's Y-Combinator in the early 2000's. This chapter demonstrates the change in character of venture capital over the period, from the occasional investment in the 1950's/1960's where venture capital took as much as 80 per cent of the equity, to venture capital in the 2000's by Y-Combinator which takes 6 per cent of the equity. While the early venture enterprises often had management control of these startups, Y-Combinator generally does not bother.

The next chapter returns to an early question "Do entrepreneurs create wealth"? Yes. The reason they do is that entrepreneurs operate under increasing returns to scale. As such they operate under the marginal revenue curve, and as long as they continue to operate under increasing returns to scale they continue to make profits, and create wealth. Since this entrepreneurial firm conducts generally a new activity, profits are not taken from other firms, but are newly created, out of nothing so as to speak. This new wealth not only benefits the entrepreneur, but society as a whole.

We then go onto to the core and the birth of an enterprise, the Idea. "In the beginning was the Idea...". This chapter states that all human development starts with the idea, and then goes on to describe a methodology to obtain valuable and productive ideas. The process is described in the book *The Idea Hunter* by Andy Boynton, Bill Fischer and William Bole. You start out considering an area that you are most interested and familiar with, your "gig". The book then goes on to use the mnemonic IDEA to hang the practical advice on how to create ideas.

Finally, we return to the adapted form of Romer's model. The model is rearranged so as to obtain a value for E, the Enterprise Quotient, which is

$$E = \frac{\dot{A_t}}{A_t \, H_{At}}$$

The value of the Enterprise Quotient E is the flow of ideas divided by the product of the stock of ideas time the amount of human capital devoted to research.

In order to get useful results, these variables were converted to suitable proxies.

$\dot{A_t} / A_t$ was assumed to be

$$B = \frac{\dot{A_t}}{\text{population}}, \quad \text{and}$$

H_{At} was converted into the ratio

$$C = H_{At} / GDP$$

The Enterprise Quotient was thus

$$E = B/C$$

A list of results was calculated. It was found from the sample that Japan had the largest Enterprise Quotient, followed by India with the second largest, beating the United States at third largest. Those countries that had the largest research effort did not necessarily have the highest Enterprise Quotient.

CONCLUSION

THE SOURCE OF ALL WEALTH IS ENTERPRISE

The source of all wealth is enterprise. Enterprise is the activity of the entrepreneur, who starts firms and sets them running in the hope for a large financial return. These firms will be profitable from the start if the operate under increasing returns to scale, and remain profitable while they continue to operate under increasing returns to scale. The firms would cease growing soon after they hit decreasing returns to scale (caused by faults in internal management), or as Adam Smith said, they hit the limits of the market.

In the first part of the book I showed that much of standard economic theory is fallacious, first in the general acceptance of the simple Supply/Demand diagram, and second the general refusal to accept the overwhelming role of increasing returns to scale, while remaining hidebound to the concept of the virtually non-existent constant returns to scale. Economic theory is not only fundamentally erroneous at a basic level, but has held back economic development and the general growth of wealth by holding these erroneous theoretical concepts.

Whether or not the reader is concerned with the state of economic theory, the reader's eyes should be opened by this book describing how the reader can get rich, by being informed regarding how easy it is to create new wealth for themselves and through that, create new wealth for the community as a whole.

146

I wish the reader good fortune in his/her pursuit of entrepreneurial wealth, and I hope he/she benefits greatly from reading this book and by absorbing the message.

APPENDIX 1

PROOF: THE MARGINAL COST CURVE IS THE SUPPLY CURVE

When the firms are competitive i.e. they act as a price taker, they take their supply decisions by maximizing the profits .

Taking price p as given:

$\text{Max}_q \ pq - C(q)$

where q is the quantity and $C(q)$ is the cost function of the firm.

The solution to the above problem is known as the supply at price p. The solution can vary with price p.

The set of all ordered pairs of equilibrium quantities with the corresponding prices is known as the supply function.

Under standard assumptions on cost functions such as: it is increasing, continuously differentiable and strictly convex, and satisfy

$\lim_{q \to 0} C'(q) = 0$

and

$\lim_{q \to \infty} C'(q) = \infty$

the solution to the profit maximization problem (supply) will satisfy:

$$p = C'(q)$$

So, (q,p) such that $p = C'(q)$ is the supply curve, and $(q, C'(q))$ is the marginal cost curve.

But since $p = C'(q)$, they are the same.

BIBLIOGRAPHY

Arthur, W Brian, (1994), Increasing Returns and Path Dependence in the Economy, The University of Michigan Press, Ann Arbor.

Baumol, William. (1968). Entrepreneurship in Economic Theory, *American Economic Review*, Vol 58, No 2, May, pp 64-71.

Beanhocher, E.D. (2006), The Origin of Wealth, Harvard University Press, Boston.

Blanchflower, D. G and A. Oswald. (1988), What Makes an Entrepreneur? *Journal of Labor Economics*, Vol 16, No1, January, pp 1-38.

Boynton, Andy, Bill Fischer, William Bole, (2011), The Idea Hunter, San Francisco, CA.

Brockhaus, Robert H. and P. Horwitz, (1986), The Psychology of the Entrepreneur, Ballinger, Cambridge, MA.

Buchanan, James M. and Yang J. Yoon, (1994), The Returns to Increasing Returns, The University of Michigan Press, Ann Arbor.

Cantillon, Richard. (1725), Essai sur la Nature de Commerce en General.

Carlsson,B. P. Branswehjebrun, M. McKelvey. C. Olofson, L. Perrsson, and H. Ylinenpaa, (2013), The Evolving Domain of Entrepreneurship Research, Small Business Economics, 41, pp 913-930.

Casson, Mark, (1982), The Entrepreneur: An Economic Theory, Barnes & Noble, Tottowa, New Jersey.

Harbison, Frederick. (1956). Entrepreneurial Organisation, *Journal of Economics,* Vol 70, No 3, August.

Hayek, F.A. (1945), The Use of Knowledge in Society, *American Economic Review*, Vol 35, No 4, September.

Keyhol, T.J., D.K. Levine, P.M. Romer, On Characterising the Equilibrium of Economics with elasticities and taxes on the solutions to the optimality problem, *Economic Theory*, pp. 43-68.

Kiyoaski, Richard. (1992), Rich Dad, Poor Dad, Time Warner Books, Los Angeles, CA.

Klein, Lawrence R. (!977). Waiting for the Revival of Capital Formation. *The World Economy*, Wiley Blackwell, Vol1 (1) pp35-46. October.

Koch, Richard, (1997), The 80/20 Principle, Nicholas Breasley, London, UK.

Knight, Frank. (1934). Risk, Uncertainty and Profit, Houghton, Mifflin and Company, New York

Lucas, R.E. (1988), On the Mechanics of Economic Development, *Journal of Monetary Economics*, 22, pp 3-42.

Marshall, Alfred (1899), Principles of Economics.

Malthus, Thomas. (1820), Principles of Political Economy.

Marx, Karl. (1867), Das Kapital.

McClelland, David. (1961). The Achieving Society, Van Nostrand, New York.

Mill, John Stuart. (1848), Principles of Political Economy.

Nelson, Richard and Sidney Winter. (1982), An Evolutionary Theory of Economic Change, Harvard University Press.

Parker, S.J. (2018), The Economics of Entrepreneurship, Cambridge University Press, Cambridge, UK.

Ricardo, David. (1817), On the Principles of Political Economy and Taxes.

Romer, Paul. (1983), Dynamic Competitive Equilibria with Externalities, Increasing Returns and Unbounded Growth, Ph.D. Thesis, University of Chicago.

Romer, Paul. (1990a), Endogenous Technological Change, *Journal of Political Economy*, 98, pp S71 – S102.

Romer, Paul (1990b), Are Nonconvexities Important for Understanding Growth? *American Economic Review*, 80(2), pp 97-103.

Say, Jean Baptiste. (1803), A Treatise on Political Economy.

Sexton, D.L and P. Kassarda, eds. (1992). The State of the Art of Entrepreneurship, PWS Kent Publishing Co, Boston, MA.

Swann, Michael and William McEachern (2006), Microeconomics: A Contemporary Introduction", Thompson, Melbourne.

Smith, Adam. (1776). Wealth of Nations.

Solow, Robert. (1956), A Contribution to the Theory of Economic Growth, *Quarterly Journal of Economics*, 70, pp 65-94.

Von Mises, Ludwig. (1949). Human Action: A Treatise on Economics, Yale University Press.

Walshaw, T. (2013), Increasing Returns to Scale, Lulu Publications, Raleigh, NC.

Warsh, David (2006), Knowledge and the Wealth of Nations, W.W. Norton & Co., New York.

Young, Alleyn. (1928), Increasing Returns and Economic Growth, *Economic Journal*, Vol 38, No 150, pp 520-542.

www.ingramcontent.com/pod-product-compliance
Lightning Source LLC
Chambersburg PA
CBHW060852170526
45158CB00001B/329